To Harry and Hope Rowe,

With real affection and all good wishes,

Samuel B. Gould

June 12, 1959

Knowledge Is Not Enough

KNOWLEDGE IS NOT ENOUGH

Samuel B. Gould

President, Antioch College, 1954-1959
Chancellor-elect, University of California, Santa Barbara

THE ANTIOCH PRESS · 1959

Some of these speeches, in whole or in large part, and sometimes in slightly different form, have previously appeared in one or more of the following publications: *Antioch Notes*; *The Antioch Review*; *Arizona Teacher*; *Association of American Colleges Bulletin*; *Association of Urban Universities Newsletter*; *California Parent-Teacher*; *Christmas Club Magazine*; *College and University*; *Highlights of the Conference on Cooperative Education and the Impending Educational Crisis*; *Journal of Higher Education*; *Louisiana Schools; The North Central Association Quarterly*; New York *Herald-Tribune*; *The Oklahoma Teacher*; *Our Reading Heritage* (Teacher's Manual, Henry Holt and Company); *The Pilot* (Elementary Classroom Teachers Association of the District of Columbia); *Pride*; *School and Society*; *Spelman Messenger*; *Student Life*; *West Virginia School Journal*; *What the Colleges Are Doing* (Ginn & Company); *Think*; United States Information Agency; *Vital Speeches of the Day*; *Wisdom.*

Acknowledgements for permission to use quotations from copyrighted material in this book are gratefully made to the American Committee for Liberation; *Daedalus* (the Journal of the American Academy of Arts and Sciences); E. P. Dutton & Co., Inc.; The Fund for Adult Education; The Kiplinger Washington Agency; *Life*; Lewis B. Mayhew; I. I. Rabi; Rutgers University Press; and the University of Toronto Press. The quotation from *The Prophet* by Kahlil Gibran is reprinted with permission of the publisher, Alfred A. Knopf, Inc. Copyright 1923 by Kahlil Gibran; renewal copyright 1959 by Administrators C.T.A. of Kahlil Gibran Estate, and Mary G. Gibran.

Library of Congress Catalog Card Number 59-11153

Printed in the U.S.A. by The Antioch Press, Yellow Springs, Ohio

To the Memory of

CHARLES FRANKLIN KETTERING

whose zeal for the proper education of youth was unquenchable during his lifetime and whose friendship, influence, and inspiration I shall never forget.

Contents

Preface

IT IS A WELL-KNOWN TRADITION, AS FORMER PRESIDENT WRISTON OF Brown once remarked, that college presidents must speak. "They must speak by day and by night, before people, before microphones, before cameras. If possible they should say something, but at least they must speak."

The chapters in this volume represent about one-quarter of the total number of speeches delivered during the last five years. They have been selected because they mirror to a large extent the educational philosophy I believe in and have been attempting to follow. They make no pretense of literary excellence. They were usually written on planes, trains, in airport waiting rooms, and in other out of the way places and circumstances. Educational journals have reprinted many in whole or in part; some have been excerpted for use in *Antioch Notes*, a modest monthly publication of Antioch College; some have been translated into foreign languages and have appeared in publications overseas.

The reader will notice that the first and larger section of the book represents talks on education made to the college community in assemblies. This is so because I have always felt the college community to be my primary and most critical audience. It has seemed to me that young people in the process of being educated should give some thought and develop some sense of commitment as intelligent citizens to the process of education itself. The second section deals more with specific aspects of the educational and administrative process and is a sampling of addresses made before various types of professional organizations.

The educational function of the college president has long been debated, particularly in recent years when the pattern of presidential leadership has been changed and even warped to meet the practical stresses of the times. More and more is being said about the president as fund-raiser, as public relations representative, or as skilful administrator. Less and less is being said about the extent to which he should exhibit educational leadership. Instead, there are those who feel that the process of shaping and developing an academic philosophy and program is not within the president's bailiwick at all, but belongs rather to the faculty alone. With these I find myself in disagreement, as this book amply illustrates.

Just how a president can exert educational leadership in view of the many other responsibilities placed upon him is a moot point. It is patently impossible for him, except in very small institutions, to be very directly involved. Yet, it appears that by being the expositor of a particular philosophy, by regularly calling attention to current educational problems, and by suggesting to his own campus ways and means by which such problems can be solved, he is fulfilling an important and even vital educational function. This may be leadership by indirection, but it is leadership none the less. The president who is silent on such issues is forgetting, it seems to me, one of the most essential components of his responsibility. This is my only defense and even apology for the number of times I have dealt publicly with the educational problems facing our nation and therefore the campuses with which I have been associated. I could not, in good conscience, do otherwise.

I should like to express my thanks to those who have been instrumental in compiling and editing this book: to Robert A. Beach, Jr. and Mildred Keenleyside, assistants to the president at Antioch College; to Paul H. Rohmann, manager of the Antioch Press; and to Dorothy High whose hours of typing were invaluable. I am also grateful to Willard M. Kiplinger of Washington, D.C., former Antioch College trustee, whose generosity has made this book possible.

SAMUEL B. GOULD

Yellow Springs, Ohio
February 1, 1959

1

New Frontiers for Higher Education

I am convinced that the tremendous and terrifying problems which now suddenly face higher education in America are the most fortunate developments ever to have occurred.

❦ ❦ ❦

We shall find in the common threads of experience which run through all cultures and make the whole world kin the material for weaving a fabric of mutual understanding.

❦ ❦ ❦

America has need of pioneers, and never more so than now. The great reaches of the continents have had their share of exploration, but the great reaches of the mind and spirit have vast unknown territories. Higher education has its portion of these unknowns, waiting only for men and women of courage and resourcefulness, experts and laymen alike, to venture boldly.

(Address at an Antioch College Assembly, January 27, 1955)

I

ONE COULD LOOK FOR NO BETTER TIME THAN THE PRESENT FOR a full re-examination of what is happening now and what seems bound to happen to higher education in America. Traditionally, our colleges and universities have placed much more emphasis upon their custodial function than upon exploring the possibilities of change and innovation. They have often indicated by their deeds that they are content to drift along, distributing the mass of knowledge they have accumulated and guarded over the years, rather than to strike out boldly into the treacherous currents formed by contemporary problems in society. Only in the area of research, both in the natural and social sciences, has higher education had moments of real magnificence. But even here it has too frequently forgotten that man has a soul as well as a personality and that he is a creature of God rather than a machine.

There is a widespread reluctance of higher education to give truly dedicated attention to the teaching process, to the development of faculty, and to the techniques which have long been proved desirable at other levels of education. Possibly brought on by some of the excessive enthusiasms of the educationists, there is still much suspicion about new-fangled notions such as audio-visual aids, or discussion groups, or integrated subject matter, or other approaches generally accepted as modern. There is a nostalgic clinging to the idea that the time-honored lecture method, the dog-eared notes which are the basis of a course year after year, the careful setting aside of parcels of knowledge into tight little compartments and departments, or even the bored graduate student in charge of an undergraduate section with half his mind on his own doctorate, the other half on the progress of his colleagues, and none at all on his students—that these are still adequate to the educational task which needs to be performed.

It is true that higher education has put a few tentative toes into the water to test the temperature and speed of the current. In its development of the concept of *general education,* it is actually up to its ankles. But it is still wading, not swimming. If the truth were told, much of what passes under the name of *general education* is merely a regrouping of an old hodge-podge of courses. The integrative process, which is the key to general education, occurs by accident, if at all.

Paradoxical as it may seem, therefore, I am convinced that the tremendous and terrifying problems which now suddenly face higher education in America are the most fortunate developments ever to have occurred. They make it mandatory for us to examine, *really* examine, what we are doing, to reassess our educational philosophy, to adopt new methods and adapt old ones, to find new resources in teachers, facilities, and financing, and in general to raise hob with the *status quo.* We shall have to solve these problems, or higher education will make a steadily decreasing contribution to the welfare of the nation, especially in the quality of its products.

Let us take a brief look at the nature and characteristics of some of these problems.

II

Over two and a quarter million young people are now enrolled in some form of higher education. Conservative estimates indicate a growth in this number by 1970 of sixty-seven per cent, or a total of three and one-half million. Add to this the fact that by 1970 a larger proportion of men and women of college age will wish to attend college, and the figure goes higher. Add also the realization that many more young people who do not attend college have the capacity to do so and that their desire will increase and will bring about modifications in admissions policies. We are told, for example, that at present about one-half our young people indicate an intelligence which would make two years of college a profitable experience for them; of these, two-thirds would probably qualify for the present four-year course. A figure of five million by 1970, therefore, is undoubtedly very conservative.

Such a rise in enrollment automatically brings with it the corresponding problems of the three F's—facilities, faculty, and financing. How will the present colleges absorb this increase in population? How will the funds be provided to expand old facilities and build new ones? Most important of all, where are we to find the teachers to staff our greatly enlarged institutions or our new ones? We have an ever-mounting shortage of qualified teachers now at all levels.

Parallel to these quantitative problems are those relating to the subject matter and methods of teaching. Is the college or university truly coming close to fulfilling its functions in society? With eighty per cent of the leadership of this country now the products of colleges and universities, how adequate is the preparation of this leadership? What are the weak spots and how can they be strengthened? Why, in the face of more and more education today for more and more people, are we unable to meet successfully the challenge of living peaceably in the world? What have we emphasized wrongly, and what have we forgotten to emphasize at all?

All these questions seem staggering to the imagination and even hopeless to consider, yet I feel that in their solution lies a new series of approaches to higher education which will vitalize the learning process, bring it into closer relationship with the contemporary scene, and add new strength and purposes. Beyond their solution lies a new educational land of exploration the frontiers of which we have not even begun to reach.

III

Only the barest mention of what we can project into the future as we think of our present educational situation is possible here. Let me sketch for you what I think the future has in store, provided we have the courage and the independence of spirit to turn our problems into opportunities. I say *we*, because all of us are involved in this, including faculty who belong to an illustrious profession in which they should rightly take pride and for which they must continue to sacrifice as never before, and including students who will soon be graduates, parents, and members of a larger community. We shall all be the ones to decide whether higher education will flourish or decline, whether it will be for many or for a few. We shall all decide the forms it will take, either letting it limp along, begging its way like a common mendicant, or supporting it willingly, even gladly.

More part-time teachers

Probably the greatest outward change of the next twenty years in higher education will be the involvement of scores and scores of educated men and women of the community to assist in the actual teaching process. It will not be possible to train (in the traditional sense of the word) all the teachers we shall need to cope with the great new influex of students, nor indeed to attract them in sufficient numbers into the profession. But it will be possible and even probable that more and more educated men and women will undertake teaching responsibilities along with their other vocations. More and more business men and industrialists will become visiting lecturers, more and more chemists and biologists and social scientists will give some of their time to the college classroom and laboratory, and more and more liberal arts graduates will find pleasure and satisfaction in exploring the humanities with the new generation. The core of full-time faculty will be the mentors and supervisors of this process, to guard carefully the quality of instruction. There is no reason to suppose that at certain levels in all areas of knowledge the quality will necessarily suffer by reason of this broadening of the faculty base.

There will, therefore, be much coming and going between the college of the future and the world around it. The responsibility for helping to staff the institutions of learning will become acutely personal to many people who have previously felt this was someone else's concern. A new and larger pooling of intellectual resources will take place, stimulated first by an emergency need but later by a realization of the advantages of such a course of action. The dynamics of education will be assisted rather than retarded.

Closer ties to the community

The college of the future will be much more closely knit to the community. Indeed, most of the new institutions which inevitably must come into being will grow directly out of the community. Their students will usually live at home. They will not have to set up an artificial college community in which to practice; they will be able to function as participants in a real community from the very beginning of their college careers without bothering about synthetic problems. And their transition from college students to adult citizenship will be virtually imperceptible.

The increasingly metropolitan character of our society will place new and unusual strains upon the urban college or university, which will find itself more and more expected to absorb the growing number of students. The great challenge of such an urban development will come in avoiding mediocrity of instruction within such a large structure. As a result, the idea of a central college with a number of branches located in strategic and nearby places will become the accepted permanent pattern just as it became a temporary pattern after World War II. Such a parent and satellite organization will keep instruction individualized, yet will offer economical administration.

The closer ties to the community will have real effect upon the traditional feelings about a college education. Much of the glamor and social prestige value will disappear, since many aspects of present campus life will be discarded as non-essential. A good deal of the social life of the student will center around the community and the college together, rather than on the college alone. In addition, the increasing proportion of young people enrolled in higher education will cause a breakdown of whatever exclusiveness remains today.

A continuing lifetime process of education

Another great change happily and inevitably will be forced upon us: a steady breakdown of the more formal lines of demarcation and division between education and life. As the college becomes more and more the cultural center of the community, there will be increased recognition that what we call "higher education" today merely supplies the tools and techniques for a continuing life-time process of education. What we now call "adult education" will become a natural and unbroken continuation of learning under the sponsorship of the college. Diplomas will represent mere check-points in this continuing process, and there will be no real segregation between the different types and levels of education. Young and old will attend classes by day or evening according to the rhythm of their own lives. Most important, students will learn at an early age that life must always be a combination of vocational and cultural pursuits. At such institutions as I am describing, the work-study plan will be obsolete in its present form but stronger than ever in a new form.

Emphasis upon leisure-time activities

It is inevitable that this emphasis upon education as a continuing process will bring correspondingly new emphasis upon the importance of leisure-time activities for the individual. It is unthinkable to assume that man must occupy all the new hours of leisure which our industrial society will make increasingly possible for him without ever using his mind. It is equally unthinkable to assume that the college will have no place in opening new avenues of exploration for him, in awakening him to new urges toward civic action and community participation, or in strengthening his bent for creativity whether it be inventive or artistic.

In the realm of physical leisure-time activities, the college will be more concerned with developing man's understanding of the natural world around him and emphasizing those play activities which can be a regular part of his adult life. The student will wish to share his interest in team sports with more individualized efforts toward general outdoor education. The opportunities for participation of the family as a unit in outdoor activities will receive added impetus and encouragement.

Development of use of mass media of communication

The mass media of communication will have a very important part to play in the college of the future. They will be the means by which the gap between home and school will frequently be bridged. They will do their share in solving the problems of teacher shortage, for new techniques of presentation will necessarily emerge involving radio, television, facsimile broadcasting, and the use of films. These techniques will not supplant the personal relationship between teacher and student which is vital to superior teaching, but they will supplement it in the areas of pure exposition of subject matter and operative procedure. They will cause great savings in time and will free the teacher to concentrate upon more creative elements in his personal relationships with the student.

We are only beginning to recognize the educational power latent in such a communication form as television, where we have in unique combination the opportunity to reach thousands or indeed millions of people simultaneously, coupled with the intimacy of approach and appeal to the individual through both eye and ear to be attained only in the face-to-face relationship of the home and seminar classroom. There are many exciting problems waiting to be solved in the field of mass media, and in their solution great implications for higher education lie dormant. Once again, the pressure upon us of the sheer weight of the numbers to be educated will force us to grapple with these problems, and eventually the nature of the college will adapt itself to this new educational tool.

Interdependence of small colleges

An interesting phenomenon of the next few decades will be the increasing interdependence of small, privately supported colleges which are reasonably close in geographic distance. The exigencies of economy will force them into co-operative arrangements so that they will share library facilities, will purchase supplies in wholesale quantities, will avoid duplication of facilities and some academic departments in some instances, and may go so far as to offer joint diplomas. By such organization they will often add great strength to themselves collectively, for they will make fullest use of the most superior qualities of their individual programs and faculties. In unity they will find added fulfillment.

IV

Up to this point, I have been discussing the college of the future in terms of its externals, the kinds of changes which will manifest themselves in new physical arrangements, new types of personnel, or in new techniques of instruction. These will be necessary and important. But they are on the plains and plateaus of adventure. The most challenging and vital frontiers to be reached lie on the ranges and mountain peaks of ideas and philosophical concepts. Let me mention only three which I think are interrelated closely and will contribute strength and power each to the others.

A global approach

I believe that the college of the future will throw off its present attitudes of insularity and will approach its teaching with a *global* outlook. It will cease giving mere lip service to "international-mindedness" by offering isolated courses in "Aspects of Western Civilization" or by sending a comparative handful of exchange students to Europe. What do we really know about the other great cultures of the world, the cultures that lie beyond the West? There are profound differences among all the peoples of the world which must be understood if there is to be any proper perspective for their associations one with the other. Today, except for an occasional "institute of African or Asiatic studies" or a course in oriental art (which merely emphasizes our piecemeal approach), we have amazingly little to be proud of in our knowledge of the East. We know little of its language and literature, and even less of its philosophy. And in some of the courses we offer in this field, we are much more directly concerned with teaching our students the potentialities of other countries as customers rather than as partners in society.

The college of the future will begin to see that the humanities are a part of all civilizations, that man's destiny lies as much in Africa or Asia or the farthest corners of the earth as it does in the cultures of our more traditional neighbors. A new all-inclusiveness will permeate the areas of knowledge to be explored, and the problems of mankind will be studied in terms of the whole human race. What Dr. Ordway Tead has called a "cultural parochialism" will be supplanted by a new awareness of what is truly meant by the word "international." We shall find in the common threads of experience which run through all cultures and make the whole world kin the material for weaving a fabric of mutual understanding.

A new sense of the spiritual quality of man

Still another idea will burgeon and spread its influence in the college of the future. I speak now of a gradual but certain awakening to the presence of a spiritual core which is central to the whole accumulation of knowledge. This will show itself most often in new and recurring emphasis upon the interdependence of man rather than in orthodoxy or denominationalism. It will often show itself by deeds rather than words. It will think of the term "*liberating*" education rather than "*liberal* education" as it realizes the need for man's soul to be free. The former is much more accurately descriptive of what we are striving for. The college will begin to ponder with greater care over the simple statement, "For what is a man profited, if he shall gain the whole world and lose his own soul?" or the sentence, "He that loseth his life for my sake, shall find it." With the study of the humanities as its central source of inspiration, the college will spread this influence into the natural and social sciences, surrounding them with a sense of mystery, of wonder, and of reverence.

The humaneness of man as a human being will take its rightful place as an object of universal concern. In his rational and spiritual qualities, he lifts himself above the rest of the animals and stands apart. It will not be enough to dissect him physically and examine his visible parts, nor to analyze his mental characteristics, unless, in so doing, there is a recognition of the great unanswerable questions which are fundamental to these analyses. The lesson which the college of the future will teach is one which was expressed back in the eighteenth century: "Knowledge is proud that it knows so much; wisdom is humble that it knows no more."

A desire for self-determination

Finally, higher education will tend to throw its support more and more in the direction of championing the capabilities of man for self-determination rather than for manipulation. The world today seems virtually obsessed with exploring the possibilities of making willing robots out of independent human beings. Soviet Russia has the most advanced techniques in this regard. But we are victims of this same sort of conditioning process here in America on a less violent scale and at a more mundane level. All our desires and emotions are played upon by master practitioners—what to eat, what to drink, where to travel, what to read—every facet of our daily lives appears to be fair game for the manipulators. We build public personalities as artfully as we build public buildings, with planned and purposeful strategy. We condition people to ideas and attitudes just as Pavlov conditioned his dogs. And somewhere in the middle of all this, the essential integrity of man and his essential capacity to determine his own destiny, to make choices, to assert his individuality have been lost or mislaid.

Socrates said that the supreme goal of education is *virtue*, "the tending of our souls," and he put to Protagoras the proposition, "I wish that you would, if possible, show me a little more clearly that virtue can be taught." Higher education has never really taken up the challenge, but has rather assumed either that the task cannot be performed or that it is not its concern. But we are stirred today as never before by the pressure of discoveries and events to an almost desperate resolve that Socrates' proposition deserves a second look. Our scientists not so long ago held to the thesis that their only function was to give mankind the fruit of their discoveries and inventions and that the use of them was someone else's problem. Today they seem troubled with the moral implications of their work.

Higher education in the future will place opposite the constantly recurring question of "*Can* we do this?" (whether it be asked in physical science or sociology or whatever else) the equally recurring and more compelling question, "*Should* we do this?" And man will have a chance to work out his own answers.

V

Well, these are some of the frontiers. I have not even touched upon others. There is, for example, the awakening of a new sense of responsibility in higher education to the needs of the superior student. There is the awakening of a new sense of responsibility to the in-service development of the teacher. And there are others. Each of the areas I have mentioned so briefly could be developed more fully, but my purpose has been to put them on the record.

It seems to me that this is the time for experimentation, for practical research in all these areas. We have a few years of grace before the full impact of population trends, technological advances, and social changes will be fully apparent. After that, it will be a mad scramble to keep up. We shall be putting fingers into the dikes against a mighty flood. In such an atmosphere of crisis we shall merely compound the errors and omissions of the past. But careful study now, properly guided and supported, will lead us to soundly conceived solutions and eventually to their implementation.

Who shall explore these possibilities? Are they valid or are they impractical dreams? If desirable, how are they to come about?

America has need of pioneers, and never more so than now. The great reaches of the continents have had their share of exploration, but the great reaches of the mind and spirit have vast unknown territories. Higher education has its portion of these unknowns, waiting only for men and women of courage and resourcefulness, experts and laymen alike, to venture boldly. The task of reaching these frontiers will have little of the heroic and dramatic to make it more appealing. Instead, it will be a stumbling, heartbreaking struggle, and its rewards will always be reaped by the generations to follow. These are, perhaps, the finest rewards, after all. At least, I like to think so.

2

Breaking the Thought Barrier

The tragedy of American education appears to be that the initial sense of wonder and the urge to explore, so characteristic in the young child, are lost in his secondary schooling and are never rediscovered during his years in higher education.

⁎ ⁎ ⁎

True education is the opposite of limitation. It differs from mere learning in that within it is an element of inventiveness. When one watches someone else perform an act and then imitates him, one may have learned a technique. But when such observation stimulates the observer to do something a different way or to think of other ideas, whether related or unrelated, then the process of education is beginning.

⁎ ⁎ ⁎

This, it seems to me, is the most pressing task of higher education today, transcending its natural preoccupation with the rising tide of students or with heavy problems of resources and facilities. Ours is the task of breaking the thought barrier which keeps our young people from realizing their creative potentiality.

(Address at an Antioch College Assembly, June 2, 1955)

I

THE MIND AND SPIRIT OF MODERN MAN HAVE BEEN STIRRED AGAIN and again in recent years as he has seen aeronautical engineers and designers devise aircraft which flew at greater and greater speeds until they succeeded in flying faster than the speed of sound. Breaking the sound barrier was indeed a magnificent achievement of modern science. But already we accept this achievement almost as commonplace and as a forerunner to new and even more compelling discoveries. Such is the swift pace that science sets for itself.

Thrilling as these milestones of progress may be, I must admit that I am just as much thrilled, if not more so, by the recent faint stirrings in the field of higher education toward what I would like to call "breaking the *thought* barrier." For example, the creative engineering course at the Massachusetts Institute of Technology is significant. General Motors Corporation and others have similar experiments in progress, all in the areas of physical science. These are a ray of hope that may possibly become a beacon, if we seriously and systematically give our attention and energy to the task of making it so.

If a text were necessary as a theme for what I have to say, it might be found in the Apostle Paul's letter to the Romans in which he counseled them: "Be not conformed to this world, but be ye transformed by the renewing of your mind." Or you might find it in Gilbert Highet's book, *Man's Unconquerable Mind*, when he says, "All important cultures . . . are manifestations of the power of the mind." Again, you might discover it in

Jacques Barzun's *Teacher in America* in which he comments, "Every college should . . . be dedicated to Intellect—not in the sense of pedantry, or verbalism, or highbrow superiority, but in the sense of Mind, free and restless in its desire to experience, comprehend, and use reality."

The physical scientist in America stands high in the regard of his fellow countrymen by reason of the tremendous range of his achievements. Even those who occasionally question his motives have no doubts about his competence and the outreach of his mind in affairs of science. But the man devoted to the humanities in America has been less highly regarded, since his creative achievements have been far less spectacular and have had far less effect upon the modern world.

A famous philosopher once said, "What is honored in a country will be cultivated there." Perhaps the new and exhilarating surge of American interest in the study of the liberal arts or the humanities is a sign that such recognition will be followed by greater cultivation. If such is the case, then the education of the *whole* man will become of equal importance to the training of the technical specialist. This may well take place, but only if we can show in the study of the liberal arts the same kind of free ranging of the mind which is becoming more and more a characteristic of the study of physical sciences.

II

Alfred Whitehead, the renowned philosopher, in his book, *The Aims of Education*, describes the education of children and young people as a movement of the mind from freedom through discipline to freedom again. The first twelve years or so of life, representing primary or elementary education, show the beginning of the mind in a phase of imaginative discovery or experience. This is a period in which the child, observing the world around him for the first time, is full of a never-ending series of questions which (to the ultimate exasperation of parents) always begin with "Why?" It is the period when as a dreamer and as a creator of imaginative visions he is filled with fantastic solutions for fantastic problems. Nothing is impossible to the child at this stage; there are no restrictive limits set by facts or experience. This disposition to explore in limitless fashion is a priceless possession of youth.

The second phase of education, corresponding with secondary education, is that of precision, according to Whitehead, in which additional facts are put in systematic order. Here is where a limiting process begins; boundaries begin to become evident, and more advanced tools of knowledge are acquired. This is followed by a third or mature stage, begun in higher education, when again there is freedom to range, but in which general ideas are developed under control of the recently imposed disciplines and highly refined techniques.

The tragedy of American education appears to be that the initial sense of wonder and the urge to explore, so characteristic in the young child, are lost in his secondary schooling and are never rediscovered during his years in higher education. Even the *theory* of returning in higher education to the imaginative and creative stage seems to have been forgotten. Somewhere along the line a stultifying process takes place, and as the child becomes a youth and then a mature person he is more and more ensnared and enmeshed in a net of factual evidence, formulæ, and patterns. This hampers his youthful daring and adventuresome spirit. What starts out in the very young as education degenerates into mere schooling—or training, if you prefer the term. The whole process becomes one of *enabling* rather than *ennobling*. It is the means of enabling the boy or girl to acquire certain techniques which will be valuable throughout life; it does not often enough concern itself with the development of the mind as an active and creative instrument, *ennobling* to the individual and to the civilization of which he is a part.

We could speculate at some length and perhaps fruitlessly about why this phenomenon has taken place. Some of the reasons may relate to the ways in which higher education is currently organized. Some may relate to the quality of instruction or even the personal desires of those who teach. We seem to have become preoccupied with a great body of knowledge as an end rather than as a means. We seem occasionally to have forgotten that cluttering up the mind with great masses of factual information is apt to be a poor substitute for the knowledge of where to find such facts when they are needed. We seem unable to separate fundamentals which *must* be taught from areas of knowledge which need only to be indicated.

Perhaps this is the reason the integrative process of education breaks down so often, for it is most difficult, if not impossible, to teach huge chunks of compartmentalized facts and simultaneously create a broad sweep of understanding in an important area of life experience. There may also be two other reasons for clinging to the traditional approach: first, the *enabling* or training portions of education are more easily measured and therefore more easily justified and defended; and second, under such a system there is very little danger that the pupil will eventually outstrip the teacher in broad grasp of the subject area.

Teachers usually look at their work from two separate and different points of view. Some consider themselves repositories of knowledge and act as dispensers of their hoard, expecting that what they have dispensed will be returned to them through examinations and recitations in good and reuseable condition. Others like to feel that they are catalytic agents, causing unpredictable changes in the minds of students, stimulating departures into unknown realms, even though this may mean, and indeed should mean, that the students will frequently return with treasure unknown even to the teacher. There are some teachers of this second category at every superior institution, but their paucity in numbers has made its mark upon the character of higher education in America.

III

If Whitehead's diagnosis is correct, the task of higher education becomes clear and unmistakable. It resolves itself into discovering the *means* by which the imaginative freedom of the child can be restored in maturity. Once discovered, these means may form the methodology for higher education.

I have already pointed out that the rudiments of such a methodology are beginning to be used in the study of the physical sciences. There are not enough indications, however, that similar rudiments have found their way into the systematic presentation of the humanities. Until they do, we are still limited in our potential range. If we are to have creative geniuses in the arts, in diplomacy, in jurisprudence, or in social science, we must take the best minds of our time and show them the possibilities of ranging far beyond the limits within which higher education so frequently restrains them.

I am not making light of the efforts of men of science in breaking the thought barrier. On the contrary, I feel that we should be grateful to them for having given us a clue to the direction all of us should be moving. But the ability of some scientists to think in new dimensions can and should have its counterpart in the liberal arts; the procedures of problem solving are amazingly similar, regardless of the type of problem.

Perhaps a few examples will show what I mean by letting the mind range freely, breaking out of the traditional circumference with which experience and education encircle it. Let me first offer two simple ones, one already solved, the other a problem which you can solve quickly. These admittedly are not at a very high level, but they may serve to show that solutions often depend upon the mind's ability to think unconventionally and not at all according to the rules. Later, I shall describe one of a higher order.

> The Creative Engineering students at the Massachusetts Institute of Technology . . . were once given the task of getting a ping-pong ball

> out of the bottom of a deep and rusty pipe that had been bolted upright to the floor. In the room with the pipe the students found hammers, pliers, rulers, soda straws, strings, bent pins and an old bucket of dirty wash water. After fishing vainly with the various tools, most of the students finally saw a solution: they poured the dirty water into the cylinder and floated the ball to the top. Then the experiment was repeated on other students with one important change: instead of the bucket, there was a crystal pitcher of fresh ice water surrounded by shining goblets on a table with a gleaming white cloth. Not one student solved the problem, because not one could connect the beautiful pitcher and its clean water with the rusty pipe.[1]

The problem for you to solve is equally simple and obvious. (I am indebted to two Detroit businessmen for this one.) Place nine circles on a sheet of paper in three horizontal rows of three, leaving some space between the rows, thus:

o o o

o o o

o o o

The problem is merely to draw, without removing pencil from paper and without going over any line twice, four straight lines which together will touch all nine circles.

More seriously, out of the recent past we can select illustrations, both dramatic and mundane, from sources other than the physical sciences, which have the marks of genius upon them. I know very little of how the plan and the technique for the writing of *Ulysses* were devised, or the concept of Lend-Lease during World War II, or the Point Four program, or the "pay-as-you-go" income tax program, or the twelve-tone musical scale. But I am certain that all of these came from minds which were thinking in new dismensions—daring, adventurous minds, will-

1. Morton M. Hunt, "The Course Where Students Lose Earthly Shackles," *Life*, May 16, 1955, p. 187.

ing to risk failure after failure in order to find ultimate success. Apparently these were minds which once given the tools of knowledge, the *enabling* elements, were still left untrammeled and with power to rove imaginatively. The problem of higher education today is one of finding the form which will guarantee that the thought barriers, heavy and thick with the barnacles of habit, will be pierced again and again. Suppose we look for a moment at what the form may turn out to be.

IV

True education is the opposite of imitation. It differs from mere learning in that within it is an element of inventiveness. When one watches someone else perform an act and then imitates him, one may have learned a technique. But when such observation stimulates the observer to do something a different way or to think of other ideas, whether related or unrelated, then the process of education is beginning. Whitehead speaks of the deadening weight of "inert ideas" in our schooling, inert because they are never, or at least rarely, the jumping-off point into new areas of creative thought. Such inert ideas frequently are buried in textbooks and need discussion and conversation between student and teacher to exhume them.

The eminent anthropologist, Robert Redfield, described in one of his lectures the record of the movements of one man's mind. Charles Darwin, in telling of his famous voyage on the "Beagle" when he was the naturalist member of a voyage of exploration and scientific observation in the South Atlantic and the South Pacific, arranged his *Journal* in two forms. One brings together matters bearing on the same topic; the other is in a form closely corresponding to his original notebooks. Redfield points out that when one compares these, one sees how Darwin's mind moved while he was in the field and something of how it moved afterward.

> It is a record of a prolonged, private and immensely productive conversation with the facts of the natural world. When it begins, the idea of natural selection was not at all present in Darwin's mind, and even the idea that species might come into being by small progressive modification, rather than by instantaneous divine creation, was hardly conceived by him as possible. When the conversation is broken off by the ending of the *Journal*, the elements of idea for the theory of natural selection are almost all present, although not yet assembled.[2]

Here is an illustration of the creative mind at work. What were some of the elements of the process which took place? First, there was the realization of the problem and the task of defining it. This was born out of a highly developed ability to observe things and to ask questions about them. The problem having been defined, the procedures of observation and questioning continued, ranging wherever they willed. They led down innumerable dead ends and into unrewarding areas, but ultimately through associative ideas they picked up a clue which led to a solution. To observe, to ask, to follow the clues wherever they led, and ultimately to solve the problem required all sorts of tools of knowledge, but they were never more than tools. As Redfield says:

> Something—an idea, a fact—is offered by a book, a teacher or the experience of life. If it flows over and past one, there is no education. If it sticks to one, and becomes training or habit, nevertheless there may be little or no education. If one deals with it, thoughtfully and reasonably, in terms of what one already is and with a result that thereafter one is by some degree more than one was before, there is surely education.[3]

V

An academic program is born out of the collective ideas of a faculty and is nurtured by the enthusiasm and dedication with

---

2. Robert Redfield, *The Educational Experience* (Pasadena: The Fund for Adult Education, 1955), p. 29.

3. *Ibid.*, p. 45.

which they address themselves to the fashioning of its parts. It is a slow, painstaking, and never-ending task, but it is the college's lifeblood just as the faculty itself constitutes the college's heart.

We all know that reorganizational changes, regroupings or eliminations of courses, and similar improvements are possible results of an examination of a college's academic program. Such a study should probe more deeply and concern itself first with the essential problem in higher education which we ought to solve. I suggest that this may be the problem of developing creative thinkers and that it may mean a most careful scrutiny of the more advanced portions of the program. I suggest, also, that it may mean a pilot experiment for a few years to see whether out of the free creative range and general formlessness or unconventionality of this educational approach may emerge a new pattern for higher education. It is for the faculty and the rest of the college community to explore all these avenues and to accept or reject the findings.

I have talked at length with many people in business, in industry, in medicine and in law, in the ministry, and in education about the values of experimentation in creative thinking in all fields. These people deserve great credit for their own creative thinking in regard to new educational horizons. They are unanimous in their desire to participate in such experimentation because they agree that it can lead to vitally important discoveries both for college and graduate school programs and later for life itself.

This, it seems to me, is the most pressing task of higher education today, transcending its natural preoccupation with the rising tide of students or with heavy problems of resources and facilities. Ours is the task of breaking the thought barrier which keeps our young people from realizing their creative potentiality.

Somewhere among the youth of today are minds capable of discovering ways to world peace, ways to deeper and more fulfilling lives, ways to new appreciations of beauty in art, or literature, or music. Just as we have already discovered minds capable of splitting the atom and delving into other abstruse scientific mysteries, so we must discover and give free opportunity of thought to those whose desire it is to make, not only a more physically comfortable or protected world, but a more spiritually centered world in which all men and nations may live with dignity.

3

A Touch of Immortality

If you have ever seen the light of understanding shine in another's eyes where no light shone before, if you have ever guided the unsteady and unpracticed hand and watched it suddenly grow firm and purposeful, if you have ever watched a young mind begin to soar to new heights and have sensed that you are participating in this unfolding of the intellect, then you have felt within you the sense of being a humble instrument in the furtherance of mankind.

Yes, a teacher is a person with a touch of immortality, and he should be most envied among men. His profession should be the most sought after, the most carefully prepared for, the most universally recognized. And, believe me, as America grows in mental and cultural stature, it WILL *be.*

(Address at an Antioch College Assembly, January 19, 1956)

WE ARE TOLD ON GOOD AUTHORITY THAT IN THE NEXT FIFTEEN years colleges and universities will require 250,000 more teachers than we have at present. This is quite apart from the even larger necessity for secondary and elementary school teachers in greater and greater numbers. Unless these needs are met, all the expenditure of money and energy on creating additional physical facilities for education will be pretty much of a waste. The log which has a student at one end and Mark Hopkins at the other may be brightly polished, enlongated, or even multiplied, but both ends of it must be occupied if education is to take place. Furthermore, the Mark Hopkins end of the log must have more than a merely physical presence. It must be populated by people having the wonderful combination of intellectual knowledge and an ability to communicate, to stimulate, and to guide. Donald Morrison, provost of Dartmouth College, has well said, "To some students, the important thing is not the subject but the teacher. In this judgment is the beginning of wisdom."

The difficulties involved in finding such people in large numbers, to say nothing of the accompanying difficulties in persuading them to enter the teaching profession and training them properly for such entrance, have been discussed countless times. Belittling the teaching profession has become part of the mores of the American people. The teacher is all too often portrayed in the American scene as a fumbling, impractical, neurotic individual living on starvation wages and seeking refuge in his profession as an escape from the world. He is the butt of many jokes, some of them rather unfunny, and he is the dupe of loan agencies or his more materially successful neighbors. He is the politician's subject of sympathetic concern only during election years. He is accused of being lazy, incompetent, sadistic, pathetic, socialistic, communistic, or in fact is labelled with any other epithet which happens to be conveniently handy except that of being rich. Indeed, Alex Drier, the commentator, says that it is wonderful to live in a country where even a street cleaner may become a college professor—at least, if he is able to make the financial sacrifice.

It is my feeling that not enough is being said in the right places to show the other side of the coin. Not enough of a case is being made in defense of the profession, and not enough is being done to change the climate of opinion. *The two parts of my thesis, therefore, are first, that the teaching profession is at least equal in importance to any other profession in the world, and second, that the liberal arts college has a vital function to perform in teacher preparation.* Unoriginal as this thesis may be, it deserves to be developed again and again, not merely at educational conferences where educators talk to one another, but on all the major platforms of the nation and particularly to young people who are considering their future careers.

It has always been a matter of profund wonder and dismay to me to note that the teaching profession makes only the feeblest efforts to show its attractiveness to young people, that it is apologetic about its position and defeatist about its future. I have listened with horror to fine upstanding teachers and guidance counselors openly warning their charges that they should avoid the teaching profession as they would a plague. I have heard them explain the financial inequities, the drudgery, the repetitiveness; and in almost every instance I have realized that the teacher was subconsciously telling an untruth, for there were any number of other career opportunities open to him if he wished to choose them. What kept him at this colorless, unexciting task when he could so easily change to something else?

A Touch of Immortality

I have had all the bitter experiences common to many teachers—financial, intellectual, social—for my teaching career began in the depths of the depression years and was marked by disappointments, privations, and insults which bordered on the fantastic. Yet I would be proud and happy if my son were to decide to make teaching his life's work. For I know in my heart, just as most of the complainers do, that there is no greater profession on earth.

Just what *is* a teacher, anyway? Having been one for years, I have naturally been curious about definitions, and I have never seen a satisfactory one. The dictionary gives very little help. It says, for example, that a teacher is "one who trains or accustoms to some action, who imparts knowledge, gives lessons in, informs, tells, makes to know how, etc." This hardly satisfies or stimulates the imagination. It is too dry, too pedantic, and most of all, too incomplete and inaccurate. My own definition, a brief one, may not be satisfactory either, but for me it comes closer to broad reality. *To me, a teacher is a person with a touch of immortality.*

Let me explain what I mean. The desire to teach is a deep-seated one and permeates the hearts and souls of thousands upon thousands who have never given conscious thought to entering the profession. We all teach in one way or another, and in such activity we find unusual and almost mysterious satisfaction. The mother and father in daily contacts with their children are teaching constantly: teaching the baby to talk; teaching the young fry to swim, to fish, to read, to sing; teaching habits of living and thinking, sometimes by precept and sometimes by example. Children teach one another at their play; colleagues in business teach one another in their professional associations; physicians try whenever possible to devote a portion of their time to teaching medical students; concert artists are drawn to young people with talent; ministers are engaged in one of the noblest forms of teaching; and so we might go on and on. Why does this happen? Because we all sense, directly or indirectly, consciously or unconsciously, that to leave a vestige of oneself in the development of another is a touch of immortality. Through this we live far beyond our span of mortal years. Through this we find new and more impelling reasons for being, for populating this earth.

If you have ever seen the light of understanding shine in another's eyes where no light shone before, if you have ever guided the unsteady and unpracticed hand and watched it suddenly grow firm and purposeful, if you have ever watched a young mind begin to soar to new heights and have sensed that you are participating in this unfolding of the intellect, then you have felt within you the sense of being a humble instrument in the furtherance of mankind. Just as the doctor feels the heartbeat grow stronger under his ministrations and is overwhelmed by the goodness and the privilege vouchsafed to him in the performance of this service for another, so each person who teaches has an awareness of this same goodness and privilege. He knows that he lives in another being, and such knowledge fills him with ineffable love and gratitude. It counterbalances all the drudgery, the heartaches, and the sacrifices which are a part of every worthwhile profession. And most of the time, because he fears being called naive or sentimental, he secretes this feeling deep within himself and says nothing about it. In fact, he joins in the brittle sophistication and cynicism of the day and uses this as a mask. But the feeling persists, all the same.

All people, particularly in youth, yearn for a career of service. This yearning unfulfilled leaves life a compromise, breeding restlessness and dissatisfaction. But when pursued unflaggingly, it creates a spiritual uplift which can take us from the morass to the stars. Think of the story of a present-day backward and illiterate nation which by the simple adoption and practice of a slogan, "Each one teaches another," has turned illiteracy into knowledge and has performed a modern miracle of teaching. What touches of immortality there were here! What devotion to service and what love of mankind! Listen to the words of Kahlil Gibran in his book, *The Prophet*:

And I say that life is indeed darkness save when
there is urge,
And all urge is blind save when
there is knowledge,
And all knowledge is vain save when
there is work,
And all work is empty save when
there is love,
And when you work with love you bind yourself to yourself,
and to one another, and to God.[1]

Yes, a teacher is a person with a touch of immortality, and he should be most envied among men. His profession should be the most sought after, the most carefully prepared for, the most universally recognized. And believe me, as America grows in mental and cultural stature, it *will* be.

II

Most of us are familiar, too familiar, with the arguments most frequently propounded to deter young people from entering the teaching profession. Suppose we examine some of these and discover how they stand up under scrutiny.

The first and most loudly proclaimed deterrent is the problem of financial return. It is pointed out that the income of teachers lags far behind that of other occupations in America. This is true. But what is usually left unsaid is that the situation is improving steadily—not dramatically, but steadily. No one will ever become wealthy through his earnings as a teacher, but the lot of the individual teacher is being ameliorated. More important, the trend is gathering momentum. It shows itself most vividly in the public schools and most specifically for the classroom teacher. Minimum standards for salaries have risen in state after state, and in many good school systems an annual salary of $6,000 or more for classroom teachers is not uncommon. It shows itself

1. Kahlil Gibran, *The Prophet*, (New York: A. A. Knopf, 1923).

least among college professors with many years of service, especially in the private institutions.

One may argue, and validly, that the years of training and study which teachers are expected to have deserve better financial recognition. But one should remember also that in many other walks of life the financial returns are not as great as one might suppose. There is a great plateau at about the $7,000 to $9,000 a year level for employees in business and industry, which only a comparative few manage to get beyond. One should also remember that the law of supply and demand will have its effect upon the teaching profession during the next fifteen or twenty years, just as it has already affected engineering and other professions.

I have not the slightest question that the next twenty years will have as a major characteristic a much more rapid adjustment of teacher salaries to meet cost of living conditions more realistically. The teacher of the future will not be affluent, but he will be paid a salary which will make possible for him the peace of mind and the dignity essential to his profession. No one with ability need fear entering the teaching profession because of its financial implications, provided that he is willing to accept the first few years as an apprenticeship during which he may not be paid as much as one starting in another profession. And even this situation may change rapidly.

Naturally, those who are primarily interested in financial gain and who are looking for ultimate salaries in the $25,000 to $50,000 bracket should not enter the teaching profession. The concept of making money for its own sake has no place in the thinking of a teacher, although there are a few teachers who have been successful in developing this concept by inordinate concentration upon their writing and consulting rather than upon their students. But I wonder how many teachers would be willing to accept along with the high salaries the competition, the pressures, the responsibilities, the insecurities, and all the other ulcer-producing characteristics which appear to go hand in hand with such financial success. I have spent enough time in the business world and in association with successful business men to be reasonably confident that not many teachers would wish to change places with them. And, parenthetically, I know many business men who look longingly at the life of the teacher.

There is a reasonable financial future for the teacher of tomorrow, assuming his ability and his progress in the profession. The more people we have who enter teaching as a means toward challenging and dedicated service, rather than as a refuge from reality, a hiatus between college and honeymoon, or a sanctuary from stress, the more rapidly will this financial future develop. Improvement in teacher quality will do much to speed and increase financial return.

A second argument presented as a deterrent to the prospective teacher is that most of the work is unmitigated drudgery. The endless series of papers to be corrected, grades to be kept in order, class preparations to be made, and other routine functions to be performed are cited as examples of deadly occupational hazards which tend to paralyze the creative urge and dry up the juices of the intellect. No one can deny that these characteristics of the profession exist, but let me point out that the same characteristics permeate every profession or occupation. There is drudgery in every calling, hours and hours of it, as many people will freely attest if they are willing to be candid. There is no profession which is a wonderful and unadulterated combination of glamor and excitement. The physician, the chemist, the lawyer, the writer, the business man, the actor—all are familiar with the hours of dull, plodding labor which is inherent in their professions.

Teaching has as much drudgery and routine in it as other professions, but no more. Its motivations are such that much of the routine dullness is forgotten in the excitement of dealing with young and developing minds. Furthermore, an increasingly intelligent attitude is evolving toward the true functions of the teacher which will, in time, relieve him of much of his present clerical burden and leave him free to give more of his time to the creative aspects of his work. People entering the profession today can do so with the hope that their expert capacities as teachers will be utilized to the fullest with mechanical duties kept at a minimum.

Another objection frequently raised against the teaching profession is that it receives comparatively little recognition and achieves little status in this country. It is argued that because material success is paramount in America, the teacher is held to be of little account. We could all offer innumerable examples of the truth of this situation, but we could also offer many examples of the direct opposite. In other words, there is nothing inherent in the teaching profession which prevents recognition and prestige. If we go unrecognized, it is largely our own fault, for we fail to follow the practical admonition of Paul, who wisely said, "I magnify mine office." As a group and individually we do little to magnify our calling; in fact, many of us take perverse enjoyment in magnifying our deficiencies. Furthermore, teachers have all too frequently withdrawn from the life of their communities and thus have been looked upon as a race apart. In instances where they have participated in community affairs, have assumed leadership in civic and cultural enterprises, and have shouldered their responsibilities as citizens as well as professional people, they have won admiration, respect, and acclaim. There is a long roster of distinguished names in government, cultural affairs, and civic activities which could be drawn up to prove the public recognition of the teacher. It ranges all the way from presidents of our country to local civic leaders. As an individual the teacher has and will continue to have all the opportunities which others have for service and prestige.

A final argument designed to make the prospective teacher hesitate is that of pointing out the great and ugly division within the profession itself. The last several decades have been marked by a great deal of suspicion and unfriendliness between the so-called "educationist" or product of a teacher-training institution, and the liberal arts college or graduate school product, who has gone into teaching without too much attention to the methodology and techniques of the profession. The teacher-training institutions, in their zeal and their enthusiasm for method, have forgotten that subject matter is at least equally important; the liberal arts colleges and graduate schools have ignored methodology and have all too frequently given us teachers who are full of their subject but unable to communicate any of it to students. Prejudice, superciliousness, supreme egotism, and unwillingness to compromise have contributed to the controversy and can be attributed to both sides. The curricula of teacher-training institutions show an appalling lack of breadth and only passing attention to content. Similarly, even though sixty per cent of those who now acquire the Ph.D. degree go into teaching, there is little if any recognition on the part of graduate schools that they have a responsibility in teacher training. The urge to teach may exist in everyone, as I have suggested earlier, but this urge needs proper strengthening by the creation of a human being with truly broad knowledge and perception, and a sensitivity to the tools of his profession.

I do not believe this schism in the teaching profession can be tolerated much longer, and there are evidences that others agree with me. I notice more and more being said and done about it, more and more efforts being made to get the two opposing schools of thought to understand one another. The realization is growing that both elements are necessary for the good teacher and that they must be provided in all institutions from which teachers will emerge.

One of the best and most immediate ways to help on the undergraduate level is to encourage students in the liberal arts to combine this work with methodology. From such a combination can come a truly prepared teacher as well as a truly prepared person. President Richard Weigle of St. John's College specifies as characteristic of the liberally educated man, "breadth of understanding, incisiveness of analysis, constructiveness and imaginativeness of thought, wisdom and cogency of judgment, clarity and effectiveness in speaking and writing. . . ." Are not all these needs of the good teacher coupled with training in the techniques of his profession? And is not the liberal arts college the proper place for the development of such a teacher? By recognizing the key position it holds, the liberal arts college can become a leader in supplying many of the thousands of teachers required for the future. A former president of Antioch College, Dr. Algo Henderson, says:

> The college is the traditional fountainhead of the knowledge that has been drawn from the accumulated experience of man, and this is the knowledge from which we expect our children to learn wisdom. Its orientation toward searching for the good life provides an educational tone of superior worth. Its congregation of students with many diverse interests in life provides a desirable environmental influence. Its dedicated faculty assures wholesome leadership and educational direction. The possibility for effectively intertwining the professional element and the liberal content for purposes of future teaching can be a distinct asset of the college.[2]

III

One final word. I have served in the teaching ranks for twenty-five years. During this time, I have watched and felt the current of opinion, understanding, and sentiment toward the teacher and his lot flow ever more surely and swiftly in the direction of enlightenment and appreciation. I tell you that the time when teachers need be apologetic and defensive about their profession is drawing to a close. The next twenty years, with their exciting struggle to solve the problems involved in educating new millions of students, will have as their inevitable by-product a changed concept of the role of the teacher and of his place in society. I say this, not as a hope, but as a prophecy.

The teacher of tomorrow will be carefully selected, broadly trained, and adequately paid. He will be the powerful force by

---

2. "Liberal Arts College and Teacher Education," *Association of American Colleges Bulletin*, XLI, No. 3 (October, 1955), 415.

which this nation will achieve the maturity of mind and the serenity of spirit that are the hallmarks of true greatness. He will have a new awareness of destiny and a new sense of calling which will undergird him as he encourages young and old in their quest for timeless truth. His eyes will be fixed upon horizons which lie far beyond geographical boundaries and which promise a new dawn of brotherhood. Most of all, he will be recognized and honored among men as one to whom God has given a priceless opportunity to serve.

This is my testament of faith in the future of the teacher in America. I earnestly invite you to join in a work which is so magnificent in its purposes, which is so deeply satisfying in its real achievements, and which bestows upon you a touch of immortality.

4

The Dimensions of a College

A college is a meeting place of ideas, jostling each other for recognition, stirring faculty and students to flights of imaginative yearning which either melt away or become hardened into practical possibility as they fall into the crucible of investigation.

✓ ✓ ✓

In seizing upon opportunities for broadening our dimension of community, we shall be broadening other dimensions of the college as well, for matters of the intellect, the spirit, and adventure are bound up in them. Successful inculcation of the concept of the never-ending nature of the educational process is the key to expanding the mental and spiritual horizons of our whole people.

✓ ✓ ✓

In the midst of day-to-day tasks, with their oppressive and wearying minutiae, it is good for us to pause and consider the dimensions of the college we are building together. And it is important for us to measure truthfully the width and depth and height of each dimension as it now stands so that we may continue to add to a structure that will never be completed.

(Address at an Antioch College Assembly, October 9, 1956)

I

IT WOULD APPEAR OBVIOUS THAT THOSE WHO DEVOTE THEIR LIVES TO the profession of education should be constantly pondering over the nature of the institutions to which they are dedicated. To be part of a college and never to give thought to the essential character and purposes of that college would be to pattern one's activities after the underground burrowings of the mole. The contemplation of the college in the wholeness of its structure is, therefore, a prerequisite for all who labor within its walls.

Nor should such contemplation be reserved to the faculty and administration alone; it is equally the duty of every student and every alumnus. The progress of our educational institutions in the future will depend very largely upon the degree of understanding of their purposes which students carry away with them into their adult lives.

If colleges and universities today, or in fact all educational institutions at every level, are not being supported as they should be, it is to a great extent because students are rarely, if ever, reminded about their responsibility for the education of others, particularly as that responsibility projects itself into the future. There is such heavy concentration by the college and the student upon himself as an individual and such attention given to his own growth as a person, that he frequently forgets to include in his scheme of life the idea of perpetuating and improving education for all in the future. Some of the least active among the proponents of better education in America are its best educated, or at least are those who have spent more years than most within halls of learning.

Yet we are witnessing a steady awakening of our nation to the problems which are plaguing the educational world. We are seeing organized and systematic efforts slowly but surely getting under way to solve the physical and personnel needs which are astronomical in their proportions. Our citizenry, or at least part of it, is becoming aroused; and we know from the history of our country that when its citizenry is aroused, things begin to happen.

As is inevitably the case when such perplexing and immediate problems face us, real danger exists that we shall forget our true reason for being perplexed. We can become so absorbed in the logistics of our problem that we lose sight of our real goal. We are not struggling to get more school facilities for the sake of getting more students comfortably under more roofs; we are doing this in order that a better trained and educated student shall emerge from under those roofs. We are not struggling merely to have one teacher for every twenty or twenty-five students in our public schools or an even lower ratio in our colleges; we are, or should be, more interested in assuring ourselves that those teachers will have competence and quality and will be proper stimulators of the abilities of our youth. Otherwise, we are due for some distressingly shoddy results.

According to what dimensions do we build a college? Everywhere in our institutions we are laboring mightily in committees, discussing, reporting, arguing, drawing plans and revising them, knocking on the doors of philanthropic organizations to support our ideas, breasting the waves of a veritable sea of mimeographed memoranda—and all for what? Why are we doing all this, doing it cheerfully, even enthusiastically? Because we know we are the architects of the destiny of our colleges, and we must build according to dimensions which can stand for generations to come. We are more fortunate than the usual architect for, as Goethe says, "How often he [the architect] expends his whole soul, his whole heart and passion, to produce buildings into which he himself may never enter." We, on the other hand, as students, as faculty, as alumni, are both architects and artisans and can live within these creations of ours as long as we like. The physical structures we build are only forerunners to our real tasks. So let us look at the dimensions of what we are building.

II

Our first concern is the *intellectual* dimension of a college. It is a dimension projected along a never-ending line which marks the search for truth, a line reaching into the infinite because we know the whole truth is ever beyond our grasp, but at the same time a line upon which we can place our feet surely and take steps toward the light of understanding. The search for wisdom through knowledge is part of this dimension, for as Socrates said, "Surely, . . . knowledge is the food of the soul," or as Shakespeare put it, "Knowledge is the wing wherewith we fly to heaven." Such knowledge, if it is to lead to wisdom, should be sweeping in its outreach, set along many and varied roads for man to explore without limitation; it should cause him to read and reflect and thus to substitute judgment for opinion; it should be rooted in an unwavering integrity which spurns the twisting of it for base purposes.

A college in its intellectual dimension should be broad enough to take in all ideas, popular and unpopular. It should be strong enough and discerning enough to recognize and to withstand the pressures of those who would pervert the college for their own expediencies, or those who guilefully use its welcome and shelter to spread their own particular brand of propaganda, and all with pious protestations in the name of freedom of speech. It should be merciful enough to suffer eccentricities gladly, yet firm enough to banish sloth and superficiality from its midst. It should be humble enough to sense the infinitesimal character of the knowledge it transmits or the wisdom it engenders by comparison with what is still unknown; at the same time, it should be proud enough to sense the true worth of its calling.

A college in its intellectual dimension should have no part of the snobbery which occasionally and unhappily becomes scholarship's masquerade and protection against the world. C. T. Bissell says quite rightly that "scholarship is the fruit of dedication and loneliness."[1] Such dedication and loneliness, however, should have the effect of developing a certain magnanimity of character as well as a desire to disseminate with clarity and simplicity the conclusions drawn from one's study and meditation. There is no place in such an intellectual dimension for the poseur, whether teacher or student, who invites the kind of bantering attack which W. H. Auden makes in his decalogue prescribed for the literary intellectual:

Thou shalt not do as the dean pleases,
Thou shalt not write thy doctor's thesis
        On education,
Thou shalt not worship projects nor
Shalt thou or thine bow down before
        Administration.
Thou shall not answer questionnaires
Or quizzes upon World Affairs,
        Nor with compliance
Take any test. Thou shalt not sit
With statisticians nor commit
        A social science.
Thou shalt not be on friendly terms
With guys in advertising firms,
        Nor speak with such
As read the Bible for its prose,
Nor, above all, make love to those
        Who wash too much.
Thou shalt not live within thy means
Nor on plain water and raw greens,
        If thou must choose
Between the choices, choose the odd;
Read the *New Yorker*; trust in God;
        And take short views.[2]

---

1. University of Toronto, *Varsity Graduate*, July, 1956, p. 127.
2. *Ibid.*, p. 127.

"The scholar," said Ralph Waldo Emerson, "is the world's eye. He is the world's heart." Besides being sharply investigative, he should be warm and responsive to all about him, even from his comparatively detached point of vantage. Out of his compassion and his urge to help, as well as out of his conviction that he must follow his inquiry wherever it leads, comes the quality of a college's intellectual dimension with room all along its lines for teachers and students alike.

III

A college should be measured next by its dimension of *adventuresomeness.* It should base its program of study upon the premise that restlessness or dissatisfaction with the *status quo* is the sign of a healthy urge toward betterment. Such an adventuresome spirit, such a desire to probe into new methods, new theories, new practices, should evidence itself in positive creativity. Here is a dimension which takes the free inquiring mind of the intellectual and sets for it exciting tasks of exploration in which the only limits are those of man's imagination. It challenges the ability to devise new forms of intellectual enterprise or new avenues of moral or spiritual inquiry.

A college is a meeting place of ideas, jostling each other for recognition, stirring faculty and students to flights of imaginative yearning which either melt away or become hardened into practical possibility as they fall into the crucible of investigation. It is a place for daring and courage, not for complacency and acquiescence. By the very definition its dimension of adventuresomeness reflects a willingness to risk or hazard in spite of our awareness that all the trial balloons will not escape being punctured or deflated. Knowledge of the past is its resource, but not its infallible guide for action.

Encouragement of the adventurous approach not only nurtures that most priceless asset of youth, creative imagination, but transmits that same asset to the faculty. In such an atmosphere mature people are constantly charged and recharged by the electrical excitement emanating from youthful restlessness and eagerness to explore. Working with young people keeps one young in heart, but only when the young people themselves are imbued with irresistible urges to meet the challenges of the time. And such an atmosphere spreads beyond a college into the community, helping to shape the latter into a more flexible pattern.

This is the kind of adventurous spirit celebrated in Joseph Conrad's magnificent story, *Youth*. You remember the tale of the old vessel, *Judea*, bound for Bangkok, and of the young second mate attached to this vessel which has everything imaginable happen to it. First it is hit by a gale just after leaving port and is almost completely disabled; rebuilt, it puts to sea again and is almost immediately rammed by another ship. More repairs and then a third try, this time in the teeth of an even worse gale than the first. The *Judea* springs a leak and all hands man the pumps hour after hour, day after day, week after week. The ship crawls into another port and then out again, with the crew rebelling because she still leaks. Back to port, and finally, with additional repairs, she heads out for Bangkok again, this time to catch fire and be abandoned with the crew taking to the long-boats. The second mate arrives in Bangkok, not as he had expected, but he arrives.

In the midst of this story is the thrilling passage in which Marlow, the second mate who is the narrator, voices what he felt as a young man when disaster after disaster was tumbling upon him:

> And there was somewhere in me the thought: By Jove! This is the deuce of an adventure—something you read about; and it is my first voyage as second mate—and I am only twenty—and here I am lasting it out as well as any of these men, and keeping my chaps up to the mark. I was pleased. I would not have given up the experience for worlds. I had moments of exultation. Whenever the old dismantled craft pitched heavily with her counter high in the air, she seemed to me to throw up, like an appeal, like a defiance, like a cry to the clouds

> without mercy, the words written on her stern: "*Judea*, London, Do or Die."
>
> "O Youth! The strength of it, the faith of it!" To me she was not an old rattletrap carting about the world a lot of coal for freight—to me she was the endeavor, the test, the trial of life.

Just as there is adventure on the high seas of Conrad's story, so is there adventure in the realm of ideas. The dimension of adventuresomeness guarantees to a college that there is no tether or hitching-post for the ideas of its constituency. It makes of the institution an exciting oasis of mental activity in the arid desert of conventional educational procedure. It opens both ends of the learning process and allows the fresh air of new ideas to blow through. "Art certainly cannot advance under compulsion to traditional forms," says Judge Augustus N. Hand, speaking of literary work, and we can add to his statement that neither can any other aesthetic or intellectual endeavor. To step boldly into the untried and unknown is the exhilarating possibility for a college with the dimension of adventuresomeness.

IV

The third dimension of a college is the *spiritual*. Of all the dimensions, this is the most intangible, the most unmeasurable, the most difficult to fit into the college's structure. It is here that we move into a greatly debated and unresolved area. How does a college teach matters of the spirit? Is it actually something about which the college should be concerned? On one side stand men like Robert Hutchins, who maintains that education of the whole man is one of the most meaningless phrases in educational discussion and that "the task of education is to make rational animals more perfectly rational." On the other side stand men like Theodore M. Greene, the philosopher, who says:

> The final test of our efforts *must* be the deepest convictions, the actual behavior, the character and lives of our students after they leave our sheltered campuses. Have we really helped them to become more alive

and sensitive, better husbands and wives and parents, better citizens, more humble and resolute and tolerant as human beings?[3]

Both men want to achieve what amounts to the same thing, but cannot agree on how to achieve it. Is it possible that all these facets of character mentioned by Greene can be acquired, as Hutchins suggests, merely by steeping oneself in the literature and accumulated wisdom of the past? Or must the college, as Greene implies, do something more to insure that its dimension of the spirit will be as great as its other dimensions? I believe it must, yet I can only grope for the ways by which it can do it. I believe the spiritual quality of a college must be its never-ending concern, regardless of how that quality is achieved.

A college's dimension of the spirit is a totality formed of many parts. Each could be the object of careful scrutiny and the basis for educational effort if a college so desired; while each cannot be "taught" in the rigid sense of the word, each can be shown to be either present or lacking in every major or minor action within the college, whether by the individual or group.

The first of these parts of the spiritual dimension is the *stature of a man's vision.* A man increases his stature as he recognizes the inadequacies of his present dreams and envisions higher ones. He increases it with the recognition of his unique potential and the use of that potential in helping to meet the world's need. We should not forget that a youth's vision is at least as much a prediction of his future as is his native endowment.

Vision alone, however, is not enough. It must be accompanied by a *dominating purpose*, developed by the person, not forced upon him. Let us not confuse this with good intentions. I am speaking of the kind of purpose which dominates one's actions. It can be measured by observing how much of what a person does consists of aimless behavior contrasted with how much goes into achieving some definite objective. It takes both vision and

---

3. "The Surface and Substance of Education," *Scripps College Bulletin*, October, 1955, p. 22.

dominating purpose to describe the forcefulness of a man's behavior. One can have vision and be a visionary, accomplishing little, or one can show much ado about very little. One who gains in college a high vision of what he wishes to achieve and bends all his efforts to that end is profiting from the dimension of the spirit provided by that college in subtle or direct ways.

The second major part of the spiritual dimension is the *force of magnanimity*. The dictionary defines magnanimity as, "loftiness of spirit enabling one to sustain danger and trouble with tranquility and firmness, to disdain injustice, meanness, and revenge, and to act and sacrifice for noble objects." The ability to rise above injustices and personal grievances is not easily obtained, but it is worth working toward. The mature individual in his daily life needs to practice both self-expression and self-renunciation many times. "He will need to learn," as one biologist put it, "that to satisfy his deepest desires he will often have to deny his most superficial desires." The urge for autonomy on the part of the individual and the urge toward magnanimity are linked together when he learns that "true freedom has to be earned and carries with it proportionate responsibilities. The dignity and importance of the individual is guaranteed only when he accepts his role in society with all its restrictions as well as its privileges."

A third component of the spiritual dimension is *faith*. I am not concerned here with defending the theological implications of faith but am content to interpret it merely as man's belief in a friendly, orderly universe. This implies a determination to search even in evil for the good it can reveal, for one believes that the good is present. Scientists, although some may not wish to admit it, also have faith. Theirs is a belief that the universe is governed by laws. It is this faith which makes them approach a problem over and over again in spite of repeated failures, never doubting that there is an answer. The great achievements of science during the last century testify to the power of such a faith.

Faith generates courage and optimism, both of which are

necessary in the spiritual dimension of a college. Certain types of physical courage are comparatively easy to inspire. The more difficult types involve years rather than moments, indefatigable patience rather than bursts of heroism, continual optimism in the face of endless discouragement, the ability to face ridicule and misunderstanding, and similarly the ability to withstand the heady wine of popular acclaim.

Perhaps a college can best teach its students in these areas by making of *itself* a continuing example in all that it does, an example of vision, dominating purpose, and faith with its accompanying courage and optimism. Then, in its spiritual dimension, it may be broad enough to foster and enlarge the vision of its students and their determination to make the conflicts among men creative rather than destructive, broad enough to keep alive their faith in something which gives them strength for this work.

V

The fourth and completing dimension of a college is that of *community*. Here is a unifying dimension both within the college itself and beyond its campus. I call it unifying because through a sense of community the college welds together the various elements of its campus population; furthermore, through the same sense it creates bonds between itself and the region where it is located. These are not the inevitable bonds of physical proximity which both region and college must accept willingly or reluctantly; they are rather the bonds which can be knit voluntarily between the two on the basis of a mutual desire to bring new cultural and intellectual enrichment to an area.

The dimension of community takes on increasing significance today as I see the mounting pressures and the impact of increasing numbers upon all levels of our educational system. Again and again I find myself reaffirming the essential goals of education, not so much because they need reaffirmation as they need to be remembered and re-emphasized. We are dedicated to an educational system based upon equality of opportunity for all, devoted to a conscious effort to develop a mature and dynamic citizenry, concerned with seeking out and strengthening the potentialities of leadership and of professional skill. Most of all, we are dedicated to a system eager to inculcate in young and old a continuing desire to learn and so to understand and enrich life generally. Such are the glorious concepts and yearnings of America.

These are our missions in education and their fulfillment will come about in many diversified ways. One of the important ways will be by the building of closer relationships between institutions of learning and the communities in which they are located. Such relationships should and will make possible our leaping over the artificial barriers to learning set up by our formal educational curricula and other structural elements and giving to all our people opportunities for individual growth which spring from their sheer joy in expanding their mental and spiritual horizons. We need all skills and abilities in America, both greater and lesser, particularly in the areas of the mind. Lyman Bryson says,

> We have never had a Western society in which there were enough places for men and women who wanted to think and could. . . . In the West we have never had any society that presented an environment adequate to develop all the potential talents and strengths in the human beings living at any moment; in developing powers of thought we have seemed to fail most tragically.[4]

It is my conviction that a college, in addition to its more readily accepted intellectual dimension which provides room for the highest kinds of scholarship and training, should have the dimension of community which offers a place for the general life enrichment of all who live nearby: young and old, artisan and farmer and member of a profession, college graduate and comparatively unschooled. Thus, many of the gaps or weaknesses which the new pressures of numbers are bound to create

---

4. *The Next America*, (New York: Harper & Brothers, 1952), p. 154.

in formal education can be filled or strengthened as a college opens its doors and its resources to all in a friendly and informal fashion, without thought of credits or degrees or anything more than to assist the burgeoning of understanding in the individual as a member of a personal, physical, political, economic, artistic, and spiritual world. Out of this dimension can come a new strength for America. It can be born of a desire to make of each community a meeting place for ideas, and fostered through the leadership of our educational institutions. It can create new and exciting uses for the great physical facilities and the intellectual or cultural resources which so many of our schools and colleges possess. Out of such a dimension can come a new unity of the people.

VI

In seizing upon opportunities for broadening our dimension of community, we shall be broadening other dimensions of the college as well, for matters of the intellect, the spirit, and adventure are bound up in them. Successful inculcation of the concept of the never-ending nature of the educational process is the key to expanding the mental and spiritual horizons of our whole people.

The time is appropriate for an even greater broadening of the dimension of community and an even greater application of the continuing education principle. The creation of a center for continuing community education, encompassing the region and with the college as the initiating force, could and should have many facets, providing varied opportunities to match the varied interests of many people. Some typical ones are listed without establishing any particular order for them or giving any details:

1. Adult education course offerings with workshops in creative writing, arts and crafts, music, courses in international affairs, the humanities, etc., to provide a program for the entire year including the summer.

2. A continuing education for alumni program wherever groups of alumni live, with the extension of such study possibilities to parents and friends of the college.

3. A summer theatre festival as an enriching experience for thousands of people in the area.

4. An FM educational radio station to broadcast fine musical and other programs to the campus, to surrounding villages, towns, and cities.

5. An alumni college in the summer with special opportunities for alumni and others to take one- or two-week non-credit courses and to participate in other cultural activities of the campus.

6. An experimental program of residential education for adults and for families, particularly on weekends and during the summer, with study, recreation, outdoor education, and general cultural benefits all a part of such a program.

7. An expanded music program to give additional emphasis upon work with the community by providing such services as music clinics and small instrumental groups.

8. A mobile theatre unit to take live theatre productions into the small towns and villages of the area.

9. Research on ways of developing attitudes and techniques necessary for the fostering of the continuing education concept among young children.

10. Training and development of leaders in the continuing education movement from among undergraduates, by courses, projects, and job experience.

There is nothing educationally fantastic or financially improbable about such a broadening of the dimension of community. Each of the items listed above, and others not listed, require study, planning, experimentation, and revision. Together they form an approach to education which this country sorely needs, an approach which gives at least a partial answer to the added hours of leisure for millions of people, the submergence of the individual in the rising tide of school enrollments, and most important of all, the yearning of each person to go as far as he can toward the goals of dynamic citizenship, increasingly humane understanding, and the general maturing and enriching of his mind. Such an approach could well be a guide for many colleges in many regions to move more surely and confidently into a relationship with their communities which would bring America closer to her dream of enlightenment for all her people.

VII

In the midst of day-to-day tasks, with their oppressive and wearying minutiae, it is good for us to pause and consider the dimensions of the college we are building together. And it is important for us to measure truthfully the width and depth and height of each dimension as it now stands so that we may continue to add to a structure that will never be completed.

Each one of us individually adds to or detracts from a college's dimensions by what we are and what we do to show what we are. We add or detract also according to the degree of our willingness to work toward the extending of these dimensions both within ourselves and in the institution. Each of us is a microcosm of the college, even though the college itself should be more than the sum of its students and faculty. Its dimensions should and can reach new heights when it is peopled and supported in its endeavors by those who work with power of intellect, with spiritual zeal, with eagerness for adventure, and with unflagging desire to serve others.

5

Maintaining a Balance in Higher Education

A new and thoroughly important aspect of our current national educational scene, an aspect which should be in your mind as well as mine, is the truly perplexing problems which beset American privately-supported colleges together as they consider how they are to be financed. Attention to this problem is vital to our individual and collective futures. Inattention to, unconcern for, and disregard of this problem by young and old in America today will lead to the greatest single tragedy the free world has ever known.

❦ ❦ ❦

We shall not bring about a strong future for America by charitably inadequate gestures or by settling for a mass education geared to the principle of mediocrity. We shall do it only by a reassessment of the true worth of education and a determination that our present diversity of pattern shall continue to exist so that everyone may be educated to the ultimate limit of his ability and motivation.

(Address at an Antioch College Assembly, January 31, 1957)

I

MUCH OF THE COLLEGE PRESIDENT'S SPARE TIME IS SPENT STUDYing and thinking about what is now happening and what lies in the future for higher education. My own studies can be placed in two categories: those which relate to the content and methodology of higher education with particular emphasis upon its value and purposes, and those which are concerned with how it is supported or is to be supported in the future if it is to survive.

I envision one extremely important and continuing duty of the college president as that of exploring with faculty and students these purposes and methods of learning as they are affected or are immutable in the contemporary scene. Such explorations should not be confined to the particular situation of an individual college, and some way needs to be found to make sure that students who graduate will emerge with a deep awareness of their own responsibilities to the cause of education generally.

Out of broad and abiding interest and understanding can come help in solving some of education's knottiest problems. Someone has well said that what happens to American education will eventually happen to America. What is thought and done ten and twenty years from now will be a key factor in whatever happens.

A new and thoroughly important aspect of our current national educational scene, an aspect which should be in your mind as well as mine, is the truly perplexing problems which beset American privately-supported colleges as they consider how they are to be financed. Attention to this problem is vital to our individual and collective futures. Inattention to, unconcern for, and disregard of this problem by young and old in America today will lead to the greatest single tragedy the free world has ever known.

II

In a recent conference dealing with civilization in the twenty-first century, Dr. John R. Weir pointed out that "the critical limiting factor on the world's resources is not materials, energy, or food, but brain power." A leading industrialist, Crawford H. Greenewalt, in a recent speech eloquently stated the need of America:

> Behind every advance of the human race is a germ of creation growing in the mind of some lone individual, an individual whose dreams waken him in the night while others lie asleep.
>
> We need those dreams, for today's dreams represent tomorrow's realities. Yet, in the very nature of our mass effort, there lies this grave danger—not that the individual may circumvent the public will, but that he will himself be conformed and shaped to the general pattern, with the loss of his unique original contributions. . . . The great problem, the great question is to develop within the framework of the group the creative genius of the individual.

The private liberal arts college is more than ever sensitive to its function in the discovery and nurturing of the kind of brain power or creative genius which these two distinguished citizens mention. It feels, as it looks around the world today, an ever-increasing need for its peculiar and even unique offering in education, emphasizing the broad and lasting values of the liberal arts and humanities which help to elevate man's mind, to keep him free in spirit, and to humanize him in his relationships with others.

American education from its very beginning has been committed to a dual competitive system of institutions financed and directed by the state and institutions financed and directed independent of the state. Roughly forty-five per cent of present-day higher education is being administered through private colleges and universities. This is a good balance and in line with the essential and desirable principle of diversity in higher education. But with the impending crisis of numbers in our educational pattern, what seems likely to happen to this balance? Let me quote two different kinds of sources for conclusions, one from the business world, the other from education.

Willard M. Kiplinger, economic and political analyst, has offered significant data and conclusions in a recent newsletter on population.

> *In college now, 3,200,000 students.* (Ten years ago it was 1,700,000)
> *In 1965, 5,200,000—60% higher.* Thus an emergency in near future.
> *In 1970, 6,700,000—doubled from now.*
>
> *How CAN colleges expand?* The private or independent institutions can expand a little but not much . . . they lack the money and the desire.
>
> *So mainly it's up to the state schools, colleges, universities,* supported by tax money. But even some of them can't expand fast enough, for they don't have the space. Besides they may get too big and unwieldy. *The answer seems to be in branches of the state universities,* located in various convenient populous areas around through the state. *Also in 2-year or junior colleges . . . local . . . locally operated . . .* "higher high schools" . . . cheaper in money and time than the regular colleges. In 1930 there were 300 junior colleges . . . now there are more than 500.

F. L. Wormald, a member of the staff of the Association of American Colleges, made a study of the enrollment plans for the next fifteen years of 515 institutions of all types but all having four-year undergraduate courses in the liberal arts and sciences. Here are two of his conclusions:

> If the growing demand for "higher education" be assumed to represent a demand for *the same kinds of education in the same proportions as obtained at present*, the four-year liberal arts colleges can as a whole take care of rather less than half of their share of the increase, unless they are furnished with additional resources not presently foreseeable.

> It appears that, in full-time undergraduate enrollments, an increase of 20 per cent across the board is all that can be expected of four-year liberal arts colleges in the next four or five years unless they obtain capital resources beyond what can now be foreseen.[1]

It is clear from the considered judgments of these two men that there will not be a place in the future for many who deserve and need the liberal arts education which the private college has to offer. This is particularly tragic when we remember that even today there is a vast uncalculated number of young people, just as capable mentally as those now in private colleges, who are not attending any college. It is clear also that the tax-supported institution will move more and more into the limelight and get more and more of the total of students.

"Within a few years," as Wilson Compton of the Council on Financial Aid to Education says,

> a decision will be reached. It may be reached by affirmative action or it may be reached by inaction. A decision by inaction will be just as conclusive. Fundamentally the question is: Do the people of the United States regard the continuance of our diversified dual system of higher education as of sufficient importance to provide it *voluntarily* the necessary financial means? This is a question to which 7,500,000 college alumni, 5,000 foundations, 6,500,000 corporation stockholders, 600,000 business concerns, 90,000,000 church members and 15,000,000 members of labor unions will find the answer, and they will find the answer within the next ten years.[2]

III

The American people have a choice to make very soon from among a number of possibilities.

The first of these choices is to agree that it is desirable that fewer and fewer young men and women receive the benefits of a liberal arts college education. It means resigning ourselves to these

---

1. "Enrolment Plans for the Next Fifteen Years," *Association of American Colleges Bulletin*, XLII, No. 4 (December, 1956), 509.

2. *Proceedings of Southern University Conference*, 1956, p. 3.

conclusions: that there is only a limited amount of room for students in our present facilities, that the chances of these facilities being multiplied or expanded are very slim, and that many students will simply have to do without a liberal arts education as we presently envision it. This choice, therefore, places new emphasis upon different kinds of education—the two-year junior or community college, the vocationally- or technically-oriented institution, and the tax-supported state universities.

It is unrealistic to expect that the basic philosophy of America which urges as much education as possible for all will be discarded. This first choice makes plain that a broad liberal arts education will be available to an ever-smaller proportion of the student population. What makes this so unacceptable is the increasing realization that liberal arts education is the finest training for executive leadership in business and industry, as well as the most necessary prerequisite for properly developed scientists, engineers, and professional men and women. It is equally unacceptable because it makes no provision for the additional thousands upon thousands of superior students who would normally benefit from this kind of education, and who would derive from it the intellectual and spiritual development necessary to future civic leadership in our country and the world. No one would argue that every student should have the same kind of education, in the same amount, but it is equally dangerous to work toward a *decreasing* rather than an *increasing* number who should have the broadest kind of educational opportunity. If we are to have an "intellectual elite" (and I don't care much for this term), it should be larger and larger as our total population increases, rather than smaller and smaller in proportion.

The second choice, which leads out of the first, is to agree to the gradual submergence of the private college and to make our whole higher education structure a tax-supported enterprise with state and federal governments supplying all the needs, capital and operational funds to the institution and scholarship assistance to the individual student. The trend is already in this direction, and there are many who welcome it. I know of ninety-one different bills already introduced into this session of Congress, relating to all aspects of education, and there will be more. The most intriguing of these relate to a federal scholarship plan, the supplying of funds for establishing junior colleges, and so on. We already are leaning heavily on the federal government for loans to create physical facilities which are income-producing, such as dormitories or dining halls. Many institutions today derive a significant amount of revenue from research contracts with various branches of the federal government.

The independence and free spirit of the private liberal arts college will inevitably suffer when it must rely almost completely upon government in order to survive. The liberal arts college functions in the realm of ideas, all kinds of ideas, and there can be no compromise with the free opportunity to explore them openly and without fear. It is difficult enough to maintain this freedom as matters stand without adding the new and even more binding element of financial dependence upon the government.

We must realize, of course, that the structure of our present federal and state tax laws is such that endowment grants as a major source of new financial support to expanding higher education will continue to decrease in number and amounts. There is little or no expectation that this tax structure will be changed. We realize, also, that income from student tuitions rarely, if ever, covers more than two-thirds the total cost to the college and frequently covers much less. Contributions to make up the difference are increasingly difficult to get and depend upon literally thousands of alumni and others who are not yet fully aware of the seriousness of the situation or whose attention is focussed upon public school education. You see, then, the horns of the dilemma on which the private liberal arts college finds itself impaled. It is reluctant to turn to the federal or state government, yet its problem of support from private sources becomes steadily more complicated.

There is, however, a third choice open, consisting of three

basic elements. One or two of these elements may be unappealing to many people, at least until they have thought about them for some time. But the choice represents a possible way to provide financial stability, opportunity to absorb the increasing numbers of students deserving of a liberal education, and freedom from government involvement beyond present practices.

The first element of this choice involves not only a continuation of the support now given to private higher education by individuals, business and industrial corporations, and indeed by all of our society, but a shift in the philosophy which brings about such support. The independent college is properly grateful for the increasing number of contributors and the growing total of money provided to it by both corporate and individual giving. This has been a most heartening development of recent years.

Education is eager that contributors look more and more upon their actions as investments in America's future rather than as one out of many charitable gifts. A recognition on their part that the education of our youth is the most important single future asset of our country will change the scale of contributions. No one minimizes the importance of the various charities which we are all called upon to support annually, but education belongs in a separate category of need and on a far different level. Higher education needs and will need one billion dollars annually for some time to come. If business had given one per cent of corporate net taxable income, it would have meant $340,000,000 instead of $100,000,000 in 1954-55. One per cent is said by some businessmen to be not unreasonable.

We are not yet offering support to education with anything like the total amount we can truly afford, compared to what we are willing to spend in other ways. We spend on luxuries far more than we appear willing to spend to support education. Simply including a small item for education in our list of charities is an indication that we do not truly understand the magnitude or the fundamental influence for the future which this problem reflects.

The individual and corporate consciousness must be awakened to the urgency of this need so that giving does not stem from charitable or altruistic motives but from the hard-headed realization that a generation or two of insufficiently and improperly educated American men and women will mean, in light of present world conditions, the collapse of the democratic way of life. An education which is firmly rooted in the broadest conceptual understandings of the dignity and worth of the individual, of his destiny on earth which goes beyond the acquisition of material comforts, of his responsibility in the perpetuation of moral and ethical values—such an education will inevitably keep us from slavery of the body and spirit. To support and strengthen such education is the solemn duty of every citizen or corporate body of citizens. We shall not bring about such a strong future for America by charitably inadequate gestures or by settling for a mass education geared to the principle of mediocrity. We shall do it only by a reassessment of the true worth of education and a determination that our present diversity of pattern shall continue to exist so that everyone may be educated to the ultimate limit of his ability and motivation.

The second element of our choice is the creation of more independent colleges, either as branches of existing institutions or as new colleges developed with the joint sponsorship of a number of presently operating institutions. I say this with full realization of the problems inherent in such a move. The costs of creating new physical facilities and operating them are viewed regularly as complete deterrents to any such plan. But I would point out a few factors which argue against such pessimism. These same deterrents existed in the nineteenth century when the major number of our private colleges came into being. Where would American education be today if our forefathers had paid more attention to the hardships involved in founding new colleges and less to the urgency of the need? All over this country today there are large estates which are steadily being abandoned by their owners or which are heavy burdens upon them. These are a potential nucleus for the physical plant necessary. It is not necessary to have beautiful Gothic structures in stately and luxurious profusion in order to carry on the essential tasks of education. It is unnecessary that we hesitate to venture because endowment funds for such institutions will be almost entirely non-existent. State universities are already receiving gifts of such estates to establish branches. There is no reason why private institutions should not welcome the same kind of opportunity.

In addition to the possibility of acquiring the basis for a physical plant through an estate, it seems to me that many cities or towns which do not at present have colleges located in or near them would recognize the desirability of having such a cultural asset. They would see the advantages in inviting such institutions to establish themselves and might even provide some financial assistance to bring this about. It is not only culturally advantageous to have a college in a community in terms of the impact it has upon the whole intellectual life of the area; it is financially advantageous also in terms of the money spent annually in the community by faculty, students, and by the institution itself. Chambers of commerce, civic organizations, and others should be quick to see this and to recognize what a variety of contributions a college can make. One needs only to look at communities where colleges are now located to see the force of this argument.

The creation of new or branch liberal arts colleges goes to the heart of the present perplexing problem of how to maintain the character and quality of education in the small college under the pressures toward expansion which are besetting us more and more. Furthermore, the active interest of presently functioning colleges in the establishment of others will guarantee the quality of the institutions of the future. The new colleges need not be exact duplicates of what exists; they can incorporate in their programs the fruit of experimental thinking and action which are taking place on many campuses today. Out of such incorporation can come an equally vital group of colleges fitted to function effectively in meeting the demands of contemporary society.

The third and most crucial element of our choice involves a new philosophical approach by the individual student and his parents to their personal responsibility toward financing a college education. There will always be a need for grants-in-aid or scholarships to assist those who are in straitened circumstances. I certainly do not advocate any lessening of our efforts to make such provisions. We must always do our utmost to help guarantee an education for those who have great financial problems when we know they are deserving and represent the highest potential ability. I am deeply concerned, however, about the increasing unwillingness of students and parents to look upon the cost of education as a primary investment in the future. Our tendency is toward more and more scholarship aid, federal and private, with no thought given to the fact that beside the many intangible benefits of a college education can be placed the distinctly tangible and material ones. It is estimated on good authority that a bachelor's degree means an average increased earning capacity during one's lifetime of $120,000. Yet, few are willing to make this investment in the future by having recourse to loan funds with generous terms for repayment at low interest rates over a long period of years. People will willingly use installment methods to buy automobiles, television sets, household appliances, or to initiate business enterprises, and will sometimes pay high interest rates to do so, yet education is looked upon either as something which we must be able to pay for immediately or get someone else to do so.

A logical system for the private college to insist upon in the future is a composite of grants and loans with real balance between the two. Scholarship funds of many schools are exhausted each year without taking care of the total need, while a good portion of available loan funds lies untouched. Part of this results from the national trend toward grants rather than loans and the fierce competition among institutions for the superior students.

It is entirely within the realm of possibility that banks now existing or specially formed corporations would be willing to provide a nation-wide system of loans at moderate interest rates and on easy repayment terms either to parents or on unsecured student loans. These would be on far different terms than we normally expect banks to grant, but they should consider their share in this as a contribution to America's future. Colleges themselves should begin to offer the opportunity for students or their parents to pay for an education over a considerable number of years, perhaps beginning before entrance to college and extending for years afterward.

There is one final element to be added to our choice. It is that the student should be expected to shoulder a larger proportion of the total cost of his education, so far as operational expenses are concerned, instead of the present fifty or sixty per cent. This would eliminate the necessity for such large endowments for present or future colleges. With the continuation or expansion of the government loan program for building dormitories, dining facilities, student centers, and other income-producing facilities, and with efforts of private individuals and corporations to assist in other capital expenditures for classroom and laboratory buildings, with basic land and sometimes with buildings provided in the turning over of estates, and with the student paying a larger share of the cost even though it may take him many years to fulfill his obligation, the private college will have at least as good and probably a better opportunity than did the newly established institution of the nineteenth century.

It is probably unrealistic to expect that any single college will be able to move by itself in the directions I have indicated. A group of colleges deciding on concerted action would have enough collective strength to cause the necessary impact upon the thinking of our people. Financial institutions are much more likely to examine the possibility of their participation when a number of colleges move together toward a more balanced grant and loan structure. Individuals with property and other resources who may look kindly upon the idea of helping new or branch colleges to come into existence will be more receptive if many institutions express their concern over the need for expanding facilities in liberal arts education. I am hopeful that as sketchy and imperfect as may be the plan I have outlined, it will serve to stir interest, comment, and suggestion so that *some* plan eventually materializes.

The approach I am suggesting is perhaps a slow and arduous one entailing as it does changes in philosophy as well as in method. If the serious planning and preliminary steps are taken now, there is likelihood that we shall not be too late in our preparations to provide a sound and independent liberal arts education to a proper proportion of the increasing numbers of students in the future.

The choices of the American people are clear. They can have a system of higher education almost completely subsidized by federal and state governments, or they can have one which holds to the original and traditional belief in the values of diversity in higher education with the private liberal arts college fulfilling an important and far-reaching function within the diversified pattern. If they choose the former, independent colleges as we know them today will eventually disappear from the American scene, except for some vestigial remains. If they choose the latter, there is good reason to hope that independent colleges not only can survive, but can grow in their total numbers to exercise the same proportionate influence among the additional millions of students and to perform even more splendid services in the creation of generations of educated men and women.

6

A Turning Point in Education

There are certainly at least four realizations to which we must adjust if we are to approach the future with any real sense of the magnitude of our problems: we are aware suddenly that we have become witnesses to the opening of a new epoch in human discovery; we are aware suddenly as a people that another political power, ideologically opposed to us, may be able to surpass us; we are aware suddenly that we are committed, willingly or unwillingly, to a military and scientific race for survival; we are aware suddenly that new directions for education in America are inevitable.

We are indeed at a turning point in education. With a new era of experience awaiting us we can turn boldly and resolutely, not in imitation of the Soviet Union or any other nation, but rather in courageous experimentation which can strengthen our belief in the free mind. We can turn our resources, our energies, and our hearts toward a new conception of the place of education in the life of this republic.

(Address at an Antioch College Assembly, December 3, 1957)

I

THE LAUNCHING OF THE FIRST RUSSIAN SATELLITE IN OCTOBER OF 1957 was the signal for an unprecedented production of oratory, charges and countercharges, accusations and justifications, predictions and warnings, and a general spate of oral and written testimony ranging from the hysterical to the soothing. It was the signal also for a sudden stir of activity in the United States, official and unofficial, as the uneasy feeling began to permeate the American mind that all was not well. The conclusions one could reach from all this, and the degree of alarm one felt, depended very largely upon what publication he read or to whose voice he listened. One could be comforted or depressed as one turned from opinion to opinion, from progress report to progress report. But for the first time, many of the essential facts about the status of Russian science and of Russian education generally became known to us as a people, not because they had been a closely guarded secret, but rather because we had chosen to ignore or misinterpret them.

There is nothing new in the concept that each generation faces the most distressingly difficult time in the world's experience. Dr. I. I. Rabi, professor of physics at Columbia University and consultant to the President of the United States on scientific matters, sums up this concept succinctly and wittily when he says:

> In every decade people seem to feel that they are living through the most difficult and trying time in the history of mankind, at least that has been my limited experience of almost four decades since I began to shave. There was the first world war when we changed the

name of Hamburg Avenue to Liberty Avenue and vowed to hang the Kaiser. This war was a prelude to the roaring twenties, which was also the period of the lost generation of F. Scott Fitzgerald. The stock market crash of 1929 ended the roaring twenties and gave the lost generation something real to think about. We then come to the 1930's, the era of the New Deal and the frustrated generation. Those days of high thinking and flat stomachs ended with the second world war. For five years we had no time for neuroses because we were fighting the darkest forces of evil ever to threaten the modern world.

The last decade since the end of the war has been in some respects one of the most remarkable of all. Instead of the predicted hard times and unemployment we have, I cannot say enjoyed, but rather bemoaned a period of prosperity unequalled in history. The political divisions within the country have hardly ever been so slight. We have had the opportunity to vote for fine men in each of the major parties whose platforms were almost indistinguishable to the unpracticed eye. Compared to the conditions of life in any other civilized country we have been living in paradise.

Yet we are told, and most of us believe, that we are living in a period of crisis unequalled in history. To be cheerful and proud of our accomplishment and optimistic of the future is almost akin to subversion. To be considered objective and realistic, one must view with alarm. We seem to be acquiring a complacency of despair.[1]

In the present circumstances, and as a nation, we face many dangers in the months and years ahead, but perhaps the greatest dangers are those of losing our sense of perspective and of searching for short-term solutions to problems which have implications for the generations yet unborn. It may be that we are not yet sufficiently out of the state of shock engendered by the latest developments to be able to meditate soberly about what all this means, but we should try. We have been subjected with alarming suddenness to a series of realizations which have struck with almost devastating impact and to which we must now adjust ourselves. When I say *we*, I mean the American people generally, for there have been individuals among us who for a long time have been aware of the imminence or the presence of these

---

1. "Science and the Humanities" (Address), pp. 1-2.

developments. These individuals have tried to utter words of caution or warning, but they have been largely ignored or discredited, so that as a total people the happenings of the present day come to us almost as a revelation.

There are certainly at least four such realizations to which we must adjust if we are to approach the future with any real sense of the magnitude of our problems. I can presume to deal with the first three only generally since they are not within my province of knowledge; the fourth is the real reason for my topic. The four realizations, each of which could well be the subject of a whole address, are these:

1. We are aware suddenly that we have become witnesses to the opening of a new epoch in human discovery.

2. We are aware suddenly as a people that another political power, ideologically opposed to us, may be able to surpass us.

3. We are aware suddenly that we are committed, willingly or unwillingly, to a military and scientific race for survival.

4. We are aware suddenly that new directions for education in America are inevitable.

II

First: we are aware suddenly that we have become witnesses to the opening of a new epoch in human discovery.

We suddenly find ourselves with the ability, actual and potential, to *participate* actively in the search for answers to mysteries of the universe, to propel ourselves into outer space and to begin to probe by actual physical exploration some of these mysteries.

A little more than fifty years ago the Wright brothers opened what we then considered to be an amazing era. They lifted man off the surface of the earth with adequate controls and opened the way for him to fly through the atmosphere and even the stratosphere. How like a mere threshold this now appears when we look at what is open ahead of us! Granted that we are inured to the fact that the world changes and that one cannot go back to yesteryear, golden as it may appear in retrospect, this is a change in our thinking so tremendous that it almost crushes us with what it portends. For generations we have been content merely to look and conjecture. Now we must face the reality of new discoveries, and we must be prepared to deal with the consequences.

I wonder how many others like me, not forewarned and not scientifically oriented, had the same reaction as mine when I first heard the news of Sputnik I. It was a sense of shock, but shock which had nothing to do with Russian enterprise or Russian superiority or anything else Russian. It was rather the sudden awareness that the world to which I was accustomed, the pace of its progress, the dimensions of its outreach, the dreams and preoccupations of those who are now mature and those who are in early childhood—that all these were changed forever. It was an awareness, too, that there was something inexorable in these changes, that there was no turning away or turning back. To live in the world from now on, I thought, would require new skills, new adaptabilities, new dimensions of knowledge, new sciences, new languages and vocabularies—indeed, a whole new outer and inner man. What that man was to be was as yet beyond my comprehension. I could only feel, and my feeling was a mixture of fear and exhilaration.

Now that there has been even a little time to become acclimated to the prospect of such rapidly expanding human knowledge, it becomes increasingly apparent that the kind of outer or inner man who emerges in the future is still within our power to shape and influence. It also becomes apparent that this new crisis is in many ways like the other more minor crises Dr. Rabi described. Mankind will adjust to it just as it has adjusted to the others, and probably with even greater speed because of the necessity. The adjustments and developments which pose the greatest problems and are the most truly fascinating in the long view are those of the inner man, for herein lies the hope of a future for this planet. Shall we be able to match the new dimensions of knowledge with correspondingly new dimensions of wisdom? The question is certainly not new, but it is more pertinent than ever.

III

Second: we are aware suddenly as a people that another political power ideologically opposed to us may be able to surpass us.

We Americans have been nurtured in a tradition of superiority. We have always felt that we were best in whatever we chose to be. We have accepted without surprise and we have adhered steadily to the belief that we have the highest standard of living, the greatest industrial output, the finest educational system, the most inventive scientists, the toughest fighting men, and so on and on. There is undoubtedly truth in some of what we have believed, but we have made the mistake of forgetting that if one wishes to maintain superiority he must do so with an inner sense of humility as well as a knowledge of and a healthy respect for what others are also accomplishing. Because of this forgetfulness, we have been inclined to belittle what the Russians were doing, even though the proofs of their efforts were easy enough to discern. As a people we have simply refused to accept the possibility that with the constricting and conforming kind of political system they espouse, the Russians could come even close to matching us. We have been especially confident of our ability to stay ahead because of the comparative newness of the USSR and because it had an essentially agrarian economy which it was necessary to transform into an industrial system.

Now we have suddenly seen the errors in our thinking. We have had brought to our attention dramatically what can happen in a dictatorship when a people is either forced into or accepts willingly a singleness of purpose and a dedication to the progress of the state. We see now that the Russians are on their way to matching the material production which we have, but with a striking difference. While we perform our work with freedom of action and with an almost casual air, they go about theirs, if not fanatically, then certainly with a seriousness and a sense of direction that do not allow distractions or postponements to interfere. We see on an even greater scale the kind of efficiency of which Nazi Germany boasted and with which it managed to shake the foundations of the world.

Yet it is important to remember, as we search for perspective, that the Soviet Union in order to reach its present point of development has had to make concessions to its people which may in time change the very pattern and basis of their ideology. A recent pamphlet of the American Committee for Liberation points this out clearly:

> The Soviet regime through the years has raised literacy and thereby aroused the thirst for more freedom of inquiry and expression. Soviet industrialization brought into being vast numbers of skilled workers, engineers, technicians, scientists—and these were bound in time to claim a better life and more dignified social status. The huge Soviet armed forces gradually developed vested interests, with officers concerned for their special status, privileges and prestige.
>
> Thus, in one area after another, Soviet society became more multiple, more differentiated. The result is a rudimentary growth of individualism with which the dictatorship, however reluctantly, must try to come to terms.
>
> Today it is no longer easy to mobilize the energies of Soviet citizens by simple, sloganized appeals to ideology. Fanatic ideologies have a way of burning themselves out. The Soviet ideology, however, has been so abused as a crass tool of power that it has lost its earlier idealistic mystique. Soviet youth and workers, for example, are no longer ready to work overtime and as "volunteers" on jobs just for the glory of the revolution. Soviet students are openly cynical about Marxist-Leninist clichés. Increasingly, it would seem, people insist on personal incentives, rewards, and even rights.
>
> The dictatorship today must deal with a different population. An essentially agrarian country has changed in a generation into a country with an urban population of some 80 million. The Soviet townsman, despite the planned isolation from the outside world, has a certain sophistication, certainly as compared with yesterday's peasant. He knows about Hemingway and TV, about jazz and vacuum cleaners and the Olympic Games. He yearns for travel abroad. He is still in

awe of the state, but a host of new impressions urges him on toward the new, the untried.

To curb these new appetites for living would require the full terror of the Stalinist era. But it is unlikely that Khrushchev & Company will dare to reimpose unlimited terror, or that they would succeed if they tried. . . . Once self-expression has been cautiously allowed, it is difficult to restore the climate of all-encompassing fear. It is quite possible, therefore, that Soviet terror has met the law of diminishing returns.

The Kremlin in the next years may possibly wish to become, by easy stages, a more enlightened—and hence more efficient—dictatorship. This, of course, not because the ruling oligarchs have had a change of heart but because they are compelled to release more popular creative energy in order to operate a modern technological economy.

The question, however, is whether a totalitarian dictatorship is really capable of harnessing free energies to its service. A little liberty, far from reconciling people to tyranny, emboldens them to demand more and yet more. The dictatorship, in stimulating individual trends for its own purposes, may well be touching off processes it will be unable to control.

A rough contemporary analogy is provided by the current fate of colonial empires. Willingly or otherwise, imperial powers in this generation embarked on policies of concessions to their colonies. The hope was to fortify the colonial system by making it softer and more and more flexible. But their subjects invariably accepted the concessions as mere down payments on eventual liberation. All through history, pressures for a change of regime increased when things were getting better, but not getting better fast enough. Will the Khrushchev policy of limited concessions, similarly, prove to be too little and too late?[2]

The lesson to us is clear and obvious. Our hope does not lie in imitating the Soviet method. It lies, rather, in supplanting our present anemic dedication with a new passion to give the broadest encouragement to the individuality and creative power of the citizen, to instill in him a desire to work for the betterment of mankind generally and the enhancement of personal dignity. If this were to be the guide and motivation of our education, then unless the facts of history are completely wrong and unless human

2. "A Fresh Look at Liberation," American Committee for Liberation, November, 1957, pp. 7-8.

nature undergoes a thorough change, my wager is that some day the Russian people could be eagerly imitating *us*.

IV

Third: we are aware suddenly that we are committed, willingly or unwillingly, to a military and scientific race for survival.

Our hope for a change in the Soviet political system of the future is *one* thing; our concern over the safety of the United States today is quite another. All we need to do to recognize the seriousness of our present situation is to imagine what our reactions would have been had the British been the nation to launch the first satellite. Instead of uneasiness on our part there would have been pleasure, since we would have had no question about the British motives. We might have been disappointed not to be first, but it would not have been disappointment colored by mistrust. Every one of the long series of events marking the progress during the past eleven years of the Soviet Union as an international power has given us cause to be mistrustful and to realize that truly friendly relations are unlikely. Under such circumstances, armed vigilance is essential. The present position of scientific leadership which the Russians have gained and to which we are for the first time fully alert makes it all the more necessary to look to our defenses.

There is no question that basic scientific research in America must be fostered and encouraged as never before. There is equally no question that we can ill afford to be second-best in the development of rocketry and missile research and the resultant exploration of outer space. We must now face the incontrovertible fact that so long as we are confronted with superior achievements in these areas by a nation to whom we are ideologically opposed and in whom we place no trust, just so long must we strive to regain and thereafter to maintain our first-rank position in scientific research. This is an unpleasant and unpalatable truth, having tremendous implications for us in terms of expenditure of money and energy. It *is* the truth, none the less, and we must learn to live with it.

Scientific equality or supremacy, however, if it is aimed merely toward military prowess, is only part of the total picture. If all we can hope for is an ability to match the Russians in each new venture into outer space as a military threat or with each new missile, then there is truly little chance for the survival of civilization except through a military stalemate. When or if that day of stalemate should come, what shall we then have to offer the world which will differ from what the Russians offer? Labor-saving devices and sleek automobiles and mass entertainment and even higher material standards of living will not be enough, for all these will ultimately be within reach of the Soviet Union, and perhaps sooner than we suppose. We must be able to offer something unattainable by the Russians under their present political system, and we must prepare today for this offering of tomorrow. If we act now with wisdom and if we approach our education of youth with wisdom, we can offer to an eager world the enterprise, the freedom, and the dignity of the individual in his mind and spirit. This is the kind of race in which we are already far ahead, and we must not be diverted by present events into relinquishing the lead. We must, in fact, increase steadily the distance between ourselves and the Soviet Union in the race to show the world how free men are created and nurtured.

V

Fourth: we are aware suddenly that new directions for education in America are inevitable.

Each of the three realizations I have just discussed has presented indirect implications for education in America, and I have tried to do no more than indicate them. It is time now to deal with the more specific implications confronting us.

The first new and inevitable direction for American education is a stronger insistence than ever that regardless of their area of specialization students be given the broadest kind of backgrounds to prepare them for life itself as well as work. Those elements which promote wisdom of the mind and serenity of the spirit must not be sacrificed because of the impelling needs of science; nor should those elements of language, our own and those of other lands, be neglected lest we find ourselves communicating so poorly with the rest of the world that we are at a constant disadvantage.

We are all familiar by now with the tremendous emphasis now being placed upon science and mathematics. The shock of the Sputniks has galvanized the people into a reappraisal of how our educational system measures up in the training of scientists and engineers. Inevitably the reappraisal is based upon comparison with education in the Soviet Union. President Dwight D. Eisenhower, in his Oklahoma speech on science and national security, made such a comparison. He said:

> The Soviet Union now has—in the combined category of scientists and engineers—a greater number than the United States. And the Soviets are producing graduates in these fields at a much faster rate. Recent studies of the educational standards of the Soviet Union show that this gain in quantity can no longer be considered offset by lack of quality. This trend is disturbing. Indeed, according to my scientific advisers, this is for the American people the most critical problem of all.

Speaking specifically of the public elementary and secondary schools, the President went on to say:

> I wish that every school board and every PTA would this week and this year make one single project their special order of business: To scrutinize your schools' curriculum and standards to see whether they meet the stern demands of the era we are entering. As you do, remember that when a Russian graduates from high school he has had five years of physics, four years of chemistry, one year of astronomy, five years of biology, ten years of mathematics through trigonometry, and five years of a foreign language.

To solve the problem of developing more scientists, the President suggested "a system of nationwide testing of high school students, a system of incentives for high-aptitude students to pursue scientific or professional studies, a program to stimulate good-quality teaching of mathematics and science, provision of more laboratory facilities, and measures, including fellowships, to increase the output of qualified teachers."

No one could quarrel with the President's statement or the suggestions made, yet the disquieting element is the failure to emphasize equally the necessities for high quality teaching in fields *other* than the sciences and the encouragement of students to enter these fields also. If we are not careful, we shall find ourselves giving mere lip service to the need for broadly educated men and women while we actually spend most of our money and energy in the science areas, not only because their needs are suddenly more critical than ever, but because these areas are more tangible and measurable in terms of results. Personally, I would be much happier with a program of action based upon the kind of statement made by Marion B. Folsom, Secretary of Health, Education and Welfare, in which he said:

> Our society is ever in greater need of broadly educated men who have the intellectual ability and the moral conviction to make those difficult and oftentimes unpopular policy decisions that determine the course of mankind's advance. Those qualities increasingly require a grasp of the scientific and technological aspects of our world, and they will ever require an understanding of the great moral, philosophical, and historical truths of mankind. . . .
>
> We have to educate professional scientists and engineers in such a way that they have a broad concept of the relationship between their technical interests and their responsibilities as citizens and human beings. The man of science, as other professional persons, must be educated to the great truth that no man or group of men lives or works alone on this earth.

It will be interesting to see whether Secretary Folsom's concern for the welfare of the whole of higher education will be reflected in the programs promulgated by the federal government.

Another implication for education of which we are suddenly aware is that of the necessity for swift changes in the financial status of teachers and of education generally. Once again we find ourselves face to face with a comparison to Soviet education. We spend on education in this country somewhere between two and one-half to four per cent of the national income; the Russians spend seventeen per cent. The average annual salary for a college professor in the United States in 1957 appeared as $5,400; his Russian counterpart earns $35,000 annually and more. Even beyond the purely monetary differences are those of status in the community. In Russia the teacher is considered to be at the high point in the social scale and he is treated accordingly; in America he is frequently the object of scorn and ridicule and the butt of rather bad jokes. A philosopher has said, "What is honored in a country is cultivated there." How much honor have we given the teacher? In our preoccupation with material gain we have dealt cruel blows to those who are dedicated to teaching. In our insistence upon measuring a man according to the accumulation of his worldly goods, we have relegated the teacher to a low place on the social ladder. Yet we have done all this with uncomfortable feelings and with pangs of conscience. For in our hearts we have suspected it was wrong and dangerous. Today, as we look at world events and our immediate problems, we *know* it was wrong, and we hope the danger can be averted.

The second new and inevitable direction for education in America is a massing of resources such as we have never before envisioned to undergird and strengthen the teaching process. Doubling our present financial outlays is only a beginning, the kind of beginning that must be made without delay. It is not a question of whether or not this is an expense we can afford; the obvious fact now is that we cannot afford *not* to incur such an expense. We must now re-examine our educational problems in respect to their infinitely larger scope as well as their greater values. We must be certain that as we put more and more of our resources into the task, we are developing a proper proportion between what we spend on facilities and what we spend on the human equation. We must remind ourselves over and over that without teachers of the highest quality all our splendidly constructed facilities will have little impact upon the improvement of education. And so the process of teacher training must be re-examined and upgraded. Refresher courses must be instituted. This is already happening in the science and mathematics areas for high school teachers with the support of the National Science Foundation, but it is equally necessary for teachers in all fields. A combination of proper training and adequate incentives will make the teaching profession attractive enough to draw greater numbers of candidates than ever before, candidates among whom we should eventually be able to make judicious selection rather than accepting all regardless of merit.

Along with teachers of quality, we must fill our classrooms with every student of ability and promise we can find. Never again must we allow today's tragic situation to be repeated, a situation in which only fifty-three per cent of college-age students with an I.Q. of 120 or better actually go to college, a situation in which over thirty per cent of the *top quarter* of our high school graduates do not go on to college. The potential strength and leadership of our nation—our youth—must be sought out and developed to the fullest.

A third inevitable direction for education is that of seeing to it that every citizen reaches maturity with a basic understanding of the scientific aspects of his world. Just as we need everyone to be broadly and humanely educated, so do we need to be assured that such breadth of knowledge includes an awareness of the place of science and an ability to adjust oneself to living in the civilization of the future. In such a civilization every creature without a grasp of the rudiments of science is an ignoramus, dangerous to himself and his fellow men, unable to protect himself or assist in the protection of others, unable to comprehend the true characteristics of his life's daily requirements. The implications of this direction point specifically to our curricula in elementary and secondary schools and the degree to which we presently make certain that all students have such basic knowledge.

The fourth and final direction for education, if it is to meet today's and tomorrow's needs, is toward the development of new understandings between the scientist and non-scientist. These must go far beyond our present efforts to offer a program of general education, for example, which all too frequently amounts to pouring some of one discipline and some of another into the students' minds in whatever doses and proportions we can agree upon, and then expecting a whole man to emerge, full-flowered in his wisdom. They must recognize first of all that the sciences and the humanities stem from different traditions, and wisdom is achieved only when these two traditions can be blended. Some of the tragic failures in world affairs from which we now suffer have come about because non-scientific people have made essential decisions in a scientific age. Yet, we would be equally vulnerable were we to turn over world decisions to our scientists. We can no longer afford the dangerous luxury of two types of learning unable or unwilling to comprehend one another. The humanist must know the sciences; the scientist must know the humanities. As Dr. Rabi says:

> Wisdom is by its nature an interdisciplinary quality and not the product of a collection of specialists. . . . The scientists must learn to teach science in the spirit of wisdom, and in the light of the history of human thought and human effort, rather than as the geography of a universe uninhabited by mankind. . . . The non-scientific faculties must understand that if their teachings ignore the great scientific tradition and its accomplishments, however eloquent and elegant their words, they will lose meaning for this generation and be barren of fruit.[3]

I should like to see the two segments of a college faculty begin to take one another's courses occasionally and become better acquainted with one another, not only as people but as scholars. Out of this could grow a mutual respect and understanding and a deeper and more meaningful program, not only in general education, but in the total experience of the student. Although imper-

3. Rabi, *op. cit.*, p. 6.

fect and fumbling, this is at least one way of moving in this new and inevitable direction. We can find other ways if we search for them.

VI

We are indeed at a turning point in education. With a new era of experience awaiting us we can turn boldly and resolutely, not in imitation of the Soviet Union or any other nation, but rather in courageous experimentation which can strengthen our belief in the free mind. We can turn our resources, our energies, and our hearts toward a new conception of the place of education in the life of this republic. We can learn the lesson we should have learned long ago, that our real strength is in our minds, not in our material wealth. If we learn this lesson well, and make it our common practice, we have nothing to fear in the long view. For the creation and development of free men in a free society is still the unique contribution of the Western world in which we are leaders. With assiduous and persevering attention to this task of educating youth in the broad attributes of humane and scientific knowledge we can still hold out to present and future generations the hope of peace and goodwill for all mankind.

7

A Tree Bearing More Fruit

We are beginning to see clearly that education is not merely the development of the mind, but rather the creation of a mature personality—emotionally stable and controlled through self-discipline. We are beginning to see that true education involves a gradual but certain awakening to the presence of a spiritual core in the whole accumulation of knowledge. It means fostering an attitude of giving rather than receiving and emphasizes deeds rather than words. It makes the humaneness of man its deepest concern.

A tree bearing more fruit is a tree which has been nurtured at its roots. This is the important lesson we are learning in higher education.... The roots of the tree of higher education are fundamental ideas which exalt and strike a divine spark in the individual, fundamental attitudes which make him see himself as his brother's keeper, fundamental facets of personality which fortify him emotionally. In addition, the roots are teachers dedicated to scholarship and to the communication of knowledge, human beings who in some mysterious way have captured the secret of taking the elements of learning and out of them inculcating students with wisdom.

(Address at an Antioch College Assembly, June 5, 1956)

I

> If you will have a tree bear more fruit than it hath used to do, it is not anything you can do to the boughs, but it is the stirring of the earth and putting new mould about the roots that must work it.
>
> SIR FRANCIS BACON

OBVIOUSLY, AS WE LOOK AT EDUCATION IN AMERICA, WE LOOK TO the future. We look to a future in which higher education will be strengthened so that it is a tree bearing more fruit. Only a part of our concern is that of mere pruning of branches which can be achieved by changing a course of study here and there or shifting an emphasis in a curriculum. Our deepest concern is that of getting to the heart of our basic problems in higher education.

To see our future way clearly, we must first examine what has happened in the last hundred years. Perhaps we do not realize often enough that a series of cultural and educational revolutions has taken place in America during this time, revolutions directly connected with the growth of higher education.

The first of these revolutions created a vast system of public education such as the world had never known or dreamed of previously. While it is true that the concept of free education for all, supported by general taxation, originated much earlier than 1856, it is also true that the development of this concept to its present gigantic proportions is the product of the last hundred years. The egalitarian principle was the rallying point of the revolution; Horace Mann came to Antioch College as its first president fresh from his battle to establish this principle with unalterable firmness. The result is a huge, sprawling structure of public education providing for millions upon millions of our youth through secondary school and even reaching into the areas of higher education. Nowhere else in the free world has such a phenomenon taken place, yet it is accepted by Americans today as though it were an ordinary occurrence.

The second revolution was that which began to place heavy strictures during the last hundred years upon the inclusion of religious training in our educational institutions. Let us remember that the earliest institutions of learning in America were usually directly connected with the church. They were primarily designed to produce ministers; hence, there was no question about the place of religion in education. As our educational system developed, however, freedom to worship as one chose under the Bill of Rights was interpreted to include freedom "not" to worship. The separation of church and state, which is one of the cornerstones of our democracy, was reason enough to keep religious training out of our public schools. Although most of the private institutions of higher education can trace their origins to some religious denomination, for many the last century has brought about either a severing or a weakening of the ties with the church. Antioch is an example of this, with its beginnings under the direct influence of the Christian and the Unitarian Churches and its later independence from denominational ties.

The third revolution was one which was *truly* a phenomenon of the last hundred years. This was the wave of sentiment toward specialization and an appreciation of its benefits that bordered on idolatry. This was true particularly in the physical sciences, but it showed itself in the other areas of knowledge as well. The demands and opportunities of an industrial civilization threw a new spotlight upon the technical expert. The expansion of our way of life with its new inventions, complicated both to create and to operate, inevitably led to a concentration upon knowing a great deal about something rather than a little about many things. In medicine the general practitioner took on an obsolescent quality; in science the chemist found he could devote his life to only one small portion of the field, and ten or fifteen kinds of engineers emerged. Even in the social sciences and liberal arts, this same specializing emphasis become more and more the pattern. And the materialistic aspects of our culture grew even more important. Freedom of opportunity was much more often linked to accumulating material wealth than to acquiring wisdom.

When we look at the results of these cultural and educational revolutions, there is much evidence to reassure us, at least superficially. Professor Theodore Greene has summarized it well:

> When, in the entire history of mankind, has so huge a society been so well fed, well clothed, well housed, well mannered, good natured and well disposed to the peoples of other nations? Not only are the vast majority of us secure against abject poverty and squalor, tyranny and fear; more and more of us are able to live lives of unprecedented comfort, both physical and mental, with ever more leisure, ever-increasing longevity, and the economic resources with which to realize many of our heart's desires. . . .
>
> Much the same can be said of our over-all pattern of education. Never has a society undertaken to educate nearly all of its young people or to carry so many hundreds of thousands of them so far up the educational ladder . . . Formal education has now become one of our great American industries.[1]

These are all surface manifestations, and they appear to have been largely governed by a general philosophy of utility. America was concerned with matters of simple literacy, of preparation for the fundamental actions of citizenship, of getting men ready for their jobs. Most of all, America was concerned with having this occur to as many of its people as was humanly possible. No one would deny that America did well in all these respects.

II

I am not contending that no distinguished or scholarly work was done in America during this time. On the contrary, we can

1. "The Surface and Substance of Education," *Scripps College Bulletin*, October, 1955, pp. 15-16.

find ample evidence of splendid results in our colleges and graduate schools. My point is that the preponderance of attention was given to the more fundamental and utilitarian processes of creating a literate and technically competent population, interpreting the more abundant life more in terms of the body than of the spirit.

These cultural and educational revolutions merely took us to a threshold, and more permanently significant aspects of education remain to be explored. As Professor Rabi, the eminent physicist of Columbia University, says:

> Every generation of mankind has to remake its culture, its values, and its goals. Changing circumstances make older habits and customs valueless or obsolete. New knowledge exposes the limitations, and the contingent nature, of older philosophies and of previously accepted guides to action. Wisdom does not come in formulas, proverbs, or wise laws but out of the living actuality. The past is important for understanding the present, but it is not the present. It is in a real sense created in the present and changes from the point of view of every generation.[2]

New cultural and educational revolutions are replacing those of the last hundred years or more, differing from the old in their aims and governed by different principles. It is heartening to see that they relate more closely to what Professor Greene calls "the inner substance" of education instead of its superficialities. They come closer to answering the kinds of questions which have plagued educators for generations. For example, why are college students so frequently less rather than more intellectually curious after a year or two of college instruction? Why has the concept of education as a continuing, lifetime process never really been understood by the college graduate? What kinds of *people* are we turning out, regardless of the knowledge and training they have acquired? What sort of philosophy of life do they have? What sort of concern for their fellow men do they indicate, not only in words but in action?

2. I. I. Rabi, "Science and the Humanities" (Address).

Although I must deal briefly with the nature of these new revolutions, which promise so much for the next fifty years, I should like at least to mention them specifically. I believe higher education can scale new heights of achievement as it becomes more and more concerned with such trends and allows them to supplement or augment what has already happened.

The growing and exhilarating emphasis upon the liberal arts and the humanities is the first and possibly the most outstanding of these new movements. In the face of the ever-increasing demand for engineers and other scientific personnel, there is a steady pressure toward giving the humanities a greater role to play in the fashioning of future generations. It apparently took World War II and its aftermath to awaken the American people to the realization that the soul and spirit of man were more important than his technical skill.

Today the liberal arts colleges hold the spotlight as they have not held it in almost a century, with business and industry joining others in the recognition that even material success today demands a *whole* man, and not just a technician. The simple wisdom of the ages appears to have new meaning for us today, and we see as never before in this country the need for the liberalizing influences of philosophy, literature, history, art, music, and, in general, the study of mankind.

We must not, however, be lulled into a sense of well-being prematurely because the humanities are getting more attention today. There are already signs of danger that this new popularity will quickly wane and will be overshadowed by a new concern of the American people. This is showing itself in a steadily developing pattern which, for want of a better name, I shall call "the pattern of quantitative matching." We are preoccupied with this pattern, in education and elsewhere, and it can destroy us if we are not careful. It is the pattern which says, for example, "The Russians are turning out 50,000 engineers annually; we must turn out 50,000 engineers as quickly as possible to match them."

Let me hasten to say that I am well aware of our need for turning out engineers and scientists in order to keep pace with the Russian challenge. What I fear is that we shall soon be turning out our engineers in the same fashion as the Russians and that our engineers will become the same kinds of people as the Russian engineers. In other words, if we fall into the trap of imitating the Russians quantitatively, we shall soon forget all the qualitative aspects of education in the sciences and will have lost what is the most important difference between Russia and America.

We must never forget for even a moment that the primary job of education is to develop *people*, not technicians, and that this is not yet of particular moment to the Russians. They are still busy creating half-men, with mental characteristics installed like the component parts of an automobile and equally standardized. With people of this type it is possible, as all of us have seen, for a government to feel that it is capable of removing a public idol arbitrarily and supplanting his philosophy with another. Whether this will turn out to be quite so easy as the present Russian leaders believe remains to be seen. James Bryant Conant, former president of Harvard, has said, "Our fitness to survive the Russian challenge depends primarily on a vigorous demonstration of the vitality of our own beliefs in democracy and freedom."

We need thousands upon thousands of engineers, but they must be engineers with minds and souls so nurtured in the humanities that they understand the true meaning of their technical calling and its relationship to life itself. To them "democracy" and "freedom" will be, not mere words, but clear ideas from which they derive some understanding of the ideals toward which this country struggles. They must not be the half-men stereotypes which Russia is grinding out in tremendous numbers—able, intelligent, competent, and completely docile if not abject. The American engineer must be the product of a broad educational process which develops his inner as well as his outer self, not the product of expediency in order to match numbers with the opposition.

The renaissance of interest in liberal arts has brought about a correspondingly new concern for the fate of the superior student in higher education. We are beginning to understand that mass education alone will not guarantee for us the development of leaders who are essential to the preservation and growth of democracy. If we are to have the highest calibre of leadership in politics, in diplomacy, in the professions, or in business, then we must consciously single out our youth with the highest potential for the most intensive kind of training and personality growth. Here is a new interpretation of the egalitarian principle, or what we call equality of opportunity, which in spite of all its splendid motivations can tie us hopelessly to mediocrity if we are not careful.

Interest in the superior student is not the only revolutionary advance we see in the principle of equality of opportunity. Even more dramatic is the long overdue extension of this principle to include all races in America. Spearheaded by a reinterpretation of the law of the land by the Supreme Court, this extension opens up new vistas of opportunity for millions of people who will now make even broader and stronger their already splendid contributions to the culture and growth of America. Nor should any present and temporary difficulties in the wider establishment of this principle cause anyone to doubt that the impact of this educational revolution upon the next several decades will be immeasurable. Equality of opportunity for all is an ideal of American democracy, rather than a total reality, yet the history of the last hundred years shows tremendous progress toward the ideal. The direction is irrevocably set, and we are moving forward patiently but firmly. There is no question as to the outcome.

Another new movement in our present culture is that brought about by the tremendous development of mass communications. What makes this important, first of all, is the effect the mass media are having upon the general integration of the American people. When as many as sixty million people are subject to the same stimuli simultaneously, when there is such interchange between areas of our country of ideas, folklore, music, and other aspects of the American scene, then the so-called hinterlands with all their implications disappear. The farmer in Idaho and the apartment dweller in New York hear, see, and read the same things at virtually the same times; they become closer to one another eventually than they themselves perhaps realize. In our time more people simultaneously have witnessed on television a performance of Shakespeare's *King Richard III* than had previously seen the play in the more than three hundred years since it was first presented.

There are educational overtones to this phenomenon, most of which still remain to be explored. There are opportunities for education to use these media of communication broadly and wisely. Let us not be misled by the hours of aimless entertainment on radio and television, by the reams of trashy newspaper material, or the reels of banal moving pictures. We have tools here which have tremendous educational implications and which can give new directions to teaching.

Experiments already completed and some still going on show conclusively what can be done in and out of the classroom with films, with closed-circuit television, with radio, with other visual and aural aids. Ways are being found to overcome the major objections to these new tools, objections pointing toward their impersonality or superficiality. It is interesting that three of the most noteworthy successes in educational television presented by universities have been in the fields of religious philosophy, psychology, and critical analysis of dramatic literature. They emanated from Washington University in St. Louis, Princeton, and the University of California, respectively. Intelligent and painstaking research in the mass media can and will bring increased vitality to the teaching process without the loss of more traditional values.

One other revolution in education should be mentioned, one perhaps more apparent to those connected with non-church-related colleges. It is the beginning of a more forthright approach to the place of religion in education. The current of attitudes and opinions in higher education is running counter to the previously accepted philosophy that in non-sectarian institutions there should be little, if any, attention paid to religion. Just as we are witnessing a new wave of interest and enthusiasm in the country at large for organized religion, we are experiencing on college campuses a new awakening to the values of religious study and activity. This does not mean any break-through in the separating wall between church and state. The non-sectarian college does not urge any denominational beliefs upon its students, nor should it do so. But it is beginning to provide more and more the climate for calm and disinterested examination of the historical and contemporary place of religion in man's life.

We define liberal education so often as the type which develops the "whole" man. Does it not seem obvious that the "whole" man is not created until he has come to grips with the problem of his religious beliefs and has determined, at least tentatively, what his own personal relationship is to the religions of the world? This question is being answered in the affirmative at an ever-increasing number of colleges.

The young student who really believes in liberal arts education today is unavoidably forced to give real attention to religion. This is assuming that the person wishes to understand the world he lives in, how it became what it is, how to struggle with its problems, and how to try solving them. For every phase of knowledge he touches shows connection between itself and religion, whether it be history, physical science, music, art, or any other. Religion is, and always has been, an integral part of human life and therefore must be part of education. A new awareness of this simple fact is changing the attitude which a good part of higher education previously held of its responsibility concerning religion.

III

It is particularly noteworthy that the elements out of which these new movements in education were created differ markedly from the utilitarianism of the last fifty or one hundred years. They represent very basic changes in American thought and action, changes which are most encouraging.

One of these elements is that of integration arising from the changes in the character of our population. The original "melting-pot" concept of America is as valid as ever, but the various ethnic groups which came to this country years ago are now well along in the process of assimilation. This has helped to raise the general level of education and to cause it to set its sights higher than ever before. Furthermore, the immigrant and minority groups have developed a fierce pride in their ability to utilize the educational opportunities which America offers. Whereas first-generation Americans were preoccupied with acquiring literacy and citizenship, the second and third generations have moved steadily into the ranks of professional men and women as well as business executives. Their contributions to the fine arts have added vitality and color to the cultural aspects of our society. Now we are concerned with ways of developing deeper and more lasting understanding among these groups in our country.

This amalgamation is a clear and powerful example of the American idea of a classless nation—classless because everyone is free to move from station to station in society, dependent only upon his ability and the depth of his desire. The newcomers to this country might easily have become a group of races apart, separated by language and foreign culture and permanently assigned to an inferior status. Instead, a campaign of Americanization and of education sprang forward; there was no thought of hereditary privileges; and this process of assimilation still goes on today, prompted by devotion to the same ideal, now closer and closer to realization.

It is the hope of the Russians that we shall fail in this striving toward a classless nation, for they are well aware of the explosive force inherent in a stratified society. Their own history offers ample proof of this force. But continuous application to the task of integrating our people, of protecting and expanding the equality of opportunity both in education and in life, will give us a spiritual weapon far more potent than the mightiest bomb. The classless society which the Russians envisage for themselves is tied closely to the whims of the State and encircled with the regimentation of the public mind. The Soviet system of education, controlled completely by the government, has no place for the free market of ideas.

Another element out of which these new movements in education have been created is the attitude of humanitarianism. Increase in regard for the individual, efforts to develop total personality to the fullest, recognition of the "value of authentic quality and responsible leadership in our cultural, social, and spiritual life"—these are part and parcel of the new approaches of education in general and higher education in particular. These efforts are not yet realized, it is true; but the fact that such goals are emerging and are increasingly the major items of consideration by educators is an indication of a most encouraging trend.

For the first time, we seem to be getting beneath the outer trappings of our educational process to the problems of what is truly taking place in the minds and hearts of our youth at the point of motivation and final belief. The new interpretation of the egalitarian principle, which I spoke of earlier, still offers education for all, but now takes real cognizance of the place of *quality*. It is a recognition of Toynbee's idea that the health of a society can be judged, at least in part, by the vigor and quality of what he calls its "dynamic minority." American higher education is beginning to give real attention to that minority in order to assure itself that it will truly be dynamic.

As this new humanitarian approach develops, we are beginning to see clearly that education is not merely the development of the mind, but rather the creation of a mature personality—emotionally stable and controlled through self-discipline. We are beginning to see that true education involves a gradual but certain awakening to the presence of a spiritual core in the whole accumulation of knowledge. It means fostering an attitude of giving rather than receiving and emphasizes deeds rather than words. It makes the humaneness of man its deepest concern.

All this is beginning to stir and become visible in higher education in the new aspirations which institutions are setting for themselves and the new tasks to which they are setting their hands. George F. Kennan has defined these aspirations very simply and echoes Dr. Conant's estimate of our situation: "Our task," says Mr. Kennan, "is to develop a spiritual vitality capable of holding its own among the major ideological currents of the time." Or, as Russell Davenport has put it, "Our task is to relate ourselves to truth in a new way; to beget a new attitude of search . . . to awaken a new spirit of inquiry in which the Idea of a Free Man can become a reality for all men everywhere."

Humane learning is the clarion call of the future, and higher education must heed this call if it is to fulfill the promise of the new revolutions in culture and in education. To achieve humane learning, we must have colleges and universities devoted to the *man* and not merely to the materials with which he works. We must have institutions which will hunger after the answers to the Socratic questions of life, the truly crucial questions which ask again and again what is *good* and *true* and *beautiful* and *just* and *pious*. The answers come, as far as it is humanly possible for them to come, from a devotion to the humanities as the core of education. Out of such answers develop the quality and pattern of man's life and his dignity as a human being.

IV

A tree bearing more fruit is a tree which has been nurtured at its roots. This is the important lesson we are learning in higher education. The roots are not buildings or stadiums or fraternities or curricular departments or objective-testing or alma mater songs, or even shelves of books. The roots of the tree of higher education are fundamental ideas which exalt and strike a divine spark in the individual, fundamental attitudes which make him see himself as his brother's keeper, fundamental facets of personality which fortify him emotionally. In addition, the roots are teachers, dedicated to scholarship and to the communication of knowledge, human beings who in some mysterious way have captured the secret of taking the elements of learning and out of them inculcating students with wisdom.

Here, then, is the function of every college or university which is a branch of this tree as it grows from its budding present to its flowering future. After we are through with many of the details of study of an educational program, we can see more clearly the threads of philosophic theory which intertwine and weave themselves together to form the fabric upon which the learning process is embroidered. We are able then to state this theory in terms of immediate and unceasing efforts to put it into practice, not merely as a collection of high-sounding phrases. Then, and only then, will the work done in the next several decades be a continuing testimonial to the power and beneficence of humane learning.

8

A Time for Candor

Significant problems are solved only by significant action; significant action does not take place in an atmosphere which reflects the feeling that we need change none of our values, give up none of our luxuries, offer no more of ourselves personally and still have the educational system we need.

We must resolutely throw aside the shibboleths which have become part of the traditions of education, however sentimentally we may view them, and recognize once and for all that an educational pattern must be shaped to the needs of the total human being and the time in which he will live.

The American people must look seriously to the reshaping of their patterns of education. They must look squarely and candidly at what they now have, and, in full recognition of the extraordinary achievements of the past and the dedication of laymen and educators alike to bringing about such achievements, they must now move boldly into the most exciting, the most demanding, and the most promising future the world has ever known.

(Address at an Antioch College Assembly, January 28, 1958)

I

THE CURRENT SPATE OF WRITTEN AND ORAL COMMENTS ON WHAT is wrong or what is right about American higher education makes me reluctant to add my voice to the chorus. Surely, it would seem by now that everything worth saying has already been said, that all the contradictions of opinion and fact have already been resolved, and that the course of action for the future is patently clear. It would seem, also, that all the generalizations which became audible almost immediately after the "beep-beep" of Sputnik I have been sharpened by now into specific and practical plans.

Candor forces me to the conclusion, however, that we have not yet reached such a crystallization point, either in thought or action, about our educational problems. We appear to be rotating around our problems as though we had acquired the major characteristics of the satellites, those of emitting repetitive sounds and never coming down to earth. I say this in spite of the discussions about the importance of science and mathematics, in spite of the pleas for holding fast to humanistic learning, in spite of the angry condemnations of "frills" in modern education, in spite of the coals of fire being heaped upon the head of John Dewey and his followers or would-be followers, in spite of all the new champions of education who have become articulate in the political or business world, in spite of the splendid work reflected by the report of the President's Committee on Education Beyond the High School or the work done earlier by the White House Conference. I say this also in spite of some very specific recent events relating to education. Among the most noteworthy was the appeal to the

American people by the President of the United States for "unremitting sacrifice" to meet the challenge of the time.

Another was the President's program for the expenditure, as a non-recurring item, of a billion dollars for education over a four-year period, promptly seconded by the Secretary of Health, Education and Welfare. You will recall that this program consisted of the following elements: a state-administered system of aptitude testing beginning at junior high school level in which federal funds must be matched by state funds; a system of federal scholarships with some preference for science and mathematics, starting with 10,000 the first year, rising to a high of 40,000, then closing out as holders are graduated; fellowships, starting with 1,000 the first year, rising by 1,500 for each of the next three years, then expiring gradually; annual grants up to $125,000 each for selected graduate schools, to be matched by the institution; grants to higher institutions for programs in foreign languages; grants to be matched by the states to be used by local districts to employ additional science and mathematics teachers, to increase salaries of teachers in those fields, to purchase laboratory equipment, and to strengthen state supervisory services in science and mathematics.

We should note a number of things about the President's program both pro and con. It *does* have the advantage of being so devised that there is little, if any, danger of federal control. But it is a "crash program" which will end after four years and which places such emphasis upon the science and mathematics areas that it will tend to develop a first and second class citizenry among teachers. The non-scientist is almost completely forgotten. Second, it does not alleviate the financial condition of higher education appreciably, since nothing is said about any portion of scholarship money going directly to colleges to take care of the total cost of students' education.

It is in the light of these two events, the President's call for sacrifice and the program he recommends, that I should like to be quite candid and forthright. Since no one else, including the

President, seems willing to say directly what is meant by "unremitting sacrifice" and what the specific nature of such sacrifice should be, I should like at least to express my opinion on what appears to be required, but only for the sacrifices necessary in education, of course. In the context of such sacrifice, I should like to discuss what I think is an adequate educational program for the future, adequate in terms of changing directions as the times seem to require.

II

It is unthinkable that the American people should ever ignore a call to sacrifice. Even our comparatively short history presents ample evidence that time after time, when crises have arisen, America has unhesitatingly done what was necessary and desirable to resolve them. But in order for sacrifices to be made, there must first be some common understandings on what is truly important. In the case of education there must be broad areas of agreement on what American education is intended to achieve. The many and diverse elements of our society, including the educators, must agree on what they expect of education, if education is ever to agree on what it should provide. This involves a long and tedious process of communication but an essential one. Today, we are only in the early stages of developing enough communication to lead to such agreement or understanding. It also involves basic attitudes, points of view, and philosophies of the American people on which any specific courses of action should be based.

The first sacrifice which the American people must make for better education, therefore, is the sacrifice of the parochial point of view.

Let me quote a portion of what I think is a significant statement on the present difficulties which arise in the relationships between education and business, labor, and industry. It was prepared by Professor Lewis B. Mayhew of Michigan State University as part of a report at the thirteenth Annual Conference on Higher Education. Professor Mayhew says:

Knowledge Is Not Enough

Society is demanding that education serve larger segments of the total population. For the colleges to assume such new responsibilities requires greater financial assistance. Before this subsidy will be willingly granted, other social institutions must understand what colleges are doing and the social pressures on them to do it. As business and industry demand more and more graduates, education must know what kind of college graduate is wanted and why. . . . Similarly business, industry, and labor must discover what are and are not legitimate demands on education. For example, business and labor groups cannot expect education to inculcate certain moral and spiritual values if these are different from those practiced in the world of work. Lastly, when purposes and functions become interrelated there is danger of wasteful duplication of effort or of important needs of society being met by no institution. . . .

Such problems of relationships and functions have been difficult to solve. In spite of good intentions in education, business, labor, and the other important social agencies, a great deal of mutual suspicion exists. The schoolman feels that business stifles humanistic man in the interest of stark materialism. The laborer feels that colleges and universities are servants of the managerial classes. He points to the business and professional men on boards of trustees of colleges, to the many courses training present or future managers and to the few courses oriented toward the worker's needs. Language, accurately reflecting how men think, is another serious obstacle. . . . But even in a situation free from suspicion and with a common universe of discourse, there would be other obstacles. Education in America has been to some extent an agent of social change. Professors and their students are expected to explore every facet of human life and to scrutinize every tenet society holds. . . . Business, on the other hand, frequently interprets its role as a conservative one. Assembly lines, mass production, and advertising have all seemingly contributed to the good life. These, then, should be preserved because they have worked. Thus here are two conflicting views—progress and change, and conservation—which must be reconciled in some way. Yet education, business, labor, and industry have not been able to clarify for themselves what their essential purposes are. College faculties cannot decide whether they should train the intellect or the whole man, nor what their responsibility is for transmitting the culture to new generations. Labor has not yet settled whether it should play an important role in management. Business has not yet decided where its productive and distributive functions end and its educational and community service ones begin. . . .

What Professor Mayhew is illustrating so vividly is the parochial point of view which sees everything in its own narrow framework. Only in the past few years have we seen efforts made to develop more and more communication among these disparate elements of our society. The best of these efforts was the formation of the President's Committee on Education Beyond the High School. Here, with broad representation, it was possible to examine the needs of higher education intelligently and dynamically. But the life and resources of this committee were both limited by the Congress, and the committee is now dissolved. What is really necessary is a dozen or more such committees of a permanent nature, all over this country, meeting regularly to emphasize their concern over a common problem and steadily creating broader and broader understandings of the objectives of education for society as a whole. There is nothing in the President's proposals to the Congress which indicates that this is considered important or which allocates funds for its encouragement.

There are two other aspects of the parochial point of view which evidence themselves *within* the structure of the American educational system itself. The first is the inability, ordinarily, of the various levels or segments of education to communicate with one another. The amount of conferring which takes place today among colleges, secondary schools, and elementary schools is anything but sufficient when one considers the importance of their relationship. Our repeated failures in such communication have contributed to the development of terminal characteristics in American education at each level and a lack of continuity in philosophy or perspective. They have contributed to the name-calling and finger-pointing which occur all too often as educators vie with each other in emphasizing the deficiencies of the particular level of education with which *they* happen not to be associated. Regular and unceasing conference among college, secondary, and elementary school educators is important if there is to be proper preparation of the student in knowledge, work habits, and attitudes as he moves higher and higher up the ladder of learning. Only then can fundamental courses have meaning or admission requirements make sense. Only then can the basis be created for a better quality of teaching at all levels.

The second aspect of the parochial point of view within education is the indifference in many instances of members of college faculties to academic disciplines other than their own. The scientist and non-scientist on many campuses find little in common and are often professionally antagonistic. With both the humanistic and the scientific areas of knowledge so vital to life in the world of today and tomorrow, this division is both tragic and dangerous. It cannot continue without compounding our errors of the past. Departmental lines must be broken down wherever possible and bodies of knowledge so presented to students that they see the integrating patterns which form a total life for the individual and his world. This is particularly essential at the undergraduate level, whether or not the student is going on to graduate school. It is just as vital for the faculty as for the students; indeed, it is a precondition for the faculty if such understandings are ever to be acquired by the students.

The attack on the parochial point of view is thus one of the prerequisites to any program of change in higher education or in education generally. Funds provided by the federal government as they were provided for the Committee on Education Beyond the High School, but in larger quantity and over a much longer period of time, could serve as one of the catalytic agents for such an attack.

III

The second sacrifice which the American people must make for better education is the surrender of their present philosophy of "business as usual."

Significant problems are solved only by significant action; significant action does not take place in an atmosphere which reflects the feeling that we need change none of our values, give up none of our luxuries, offer no more of ourselves personally and still have the educational system we need.

If we look at the financial side of the picture, the question is not so much one of how much more money must be spent to assure a high quality of education. We know we must spend more, a good deal more. Rather, the question is how much more of what we now spend on *everything* we are willing to allocate to education. Colleges and universities, public and private, are currently spending three billion dollars a year which represents three-fourths of one per cent of the Gross National Product.

In order to catch up on our present shortages and to meet the demands of the next ten years, it will be necessary to double the number of faculty. Furthermore, let us realize that, according to the Council for Financial Aid to Education, the average teacher in the United States in 1956 was earning seventy per cent, in real income, of what he earned in 1940. The average factory worker was earning 150 per cent, in real income, of what he earned in 1940. If the teacher is to receive an equitable salary, therefore, and if we are to double the number of teachers, we come to the inevitable conclusion that ten years hence we must spend at least four times the amount of money we now spend on this single educational item alone. This, together with expenditures for new facilities, would represent three per cent of the Gross National Product assuming that the latter does not increase, and this would be a very pessimistic assumption. Three per cent of the Gross National Product is less than we currently spend on items such as cosmetics, liquor, cigarettes, electrical appliances, automobiles, or entertainment.

You have seen and heard dull statistics such as these many times before, I hope, but I am repeating them purposely. If I had my way, I would have them repeated to the American people every day of the year. Perhaps, then, someone might pause before buying that second or third car, the second television set, the new electrical gadget, and ask himself before doing so whether he had fulfilled his personal obligation to education. Admiral Rickover, in his statement called "The Balance Sheet on Education," puts the case bluntly:

> Ours is an enormously productive economy—the first in history which produces a large surplus over and above reasonable necessities of life. The flood of goods coming off our production lines is so tremendous that some ten billion dollars must be spent annually to encourage disposal of them. I speak of course of advertising which costs us as much as all our primary and secondary public schools put together. This is money with which advertisers finance our mass media and through them ceaselessly hammer at the need for ever more and better goods and services. People must be made to buy things for which they feel no need; they must be induced to replace possessions still entirely satisfactory for new ones which, it is promised, will make them up-to-date and keep up the family's prestige. Their subconscious is probed in order to find ways to stifle the still voice of conscience and induce the American people to go into consumer debts of over three billion dollars annually—forty-two billion standing on the books as of now. Often young children are conditioned to act as unpaid boosters for higher consumption.
>
> The automobile industry alone must spend one and a half billion dollars each year to design and bring out new models in order to insure that American families keep spending ten per cent of their income on cars. This one and a half billion dollars is about three-quarters of what the nation spends on all its public colleges and universities. I mention these figures to show that sacrifices to give America strength in the race with Russia would be insignificant in view of our enormous margin of luxury spending.[1]

The question, you see, is how badly do the American people want high quality education. Do they want it badly enough to pay for it? Or do the parents in this country expect the teachers of America to go on personally subsidizing the education of their children as they do today?

The President's proposals for education take no cognizance of this need for a change in attitude. Indeed, a component part of the proposals is a federal scholarship plan which says nothing about the additional costs of the college, and which does not raise

1. Hyman G. Rickover, *Education and Freedom* (New York: E. P. Dutton & Co., 1959), pp. 165-6.

the question of personal responsibility of the student or parent by suggesting loans to supplement the scholarship aid.

I said at the outset that I wanted to be candid and forthright on this subject, and I hope that as I do this your sensibilities will not be hurt. It is time these facts were stated in such terms that no one can possibly misunderstand. The fact is that every student in a private college or university today owes or will owe his college or university hundreds of dollars for his education by the time he graduates. This does not take into account any scholarship or tuition reduction assistance he may receive. The fact is, also, that the money he is not paying is coming directly out of the pockets of the faculty of his institution. It is their personal gift to him which they make at the sacrifice of what we normally consider necessities of life. They have less money for food, for clothing, for shelter, for recreation, for study and professional growth, for travel, for educating their own children because they have assumed his education as their personal obligation.

In order to reduce to a minimum the amount of sacrifice the faculty member is making, it is necessary for the private college president to spend a considerable amount of time searching for people and organizations who may be begged, urged, cajoled, and occasionally persuaded into providing funds to make up annual deficits. I am one who has done this willingly, but with no illusions as to what this means to my obligation for offering educational leadership to a college community. This is another one of the facts of American college life today, that college and university presidents are seen more often in the offices of businessmen and foundations than they are in the classrooms of their campuses. I have tried to make up for this kind of personal remoteness by gathering as much financial support as possible for educational ideas I believe to be important to the college and to the country, but which I have only the most limited time to explore and develop myself.

The goal we have set for ourselves in education will not be reached without sacrifice by the American people, the kind of sacrifice which impels them to put educational necessity for their children before personal luxury. That the President's program is a relatively short-term one, that it emphasizes the sciences and mathematics so heavily, and that it offers scholarships to qualified students with no mention of the students' own investment in their future are disappointing facts to some of us, but they are not too disturbing. For the real lift which education needs must come out of the minds and hearts and pocketbooks of the American people themselves. A realization on their part that education is the key to America's future and an inclination to make sacrifices to support that realization are the truly essential factors which can give us hope. The federal and state governments can and do provide assistance of many kinds, and should continue to provide it increasingly, but it is not the American way to turn the responsibility completely over to government. It is not only *desirable* to maintain the present diversity in education; it is also *feasible*, if our people have the will to make it so.

IV

A sacrifice of money, however, is not enough to fulfill the change in philosophy now so necessary. Still another sacrifice must be made. We must resolutely throw aside the shibboleths which have become part of the traditions of education, however sentimentally we may view them, and recognize once and for all that an educational pattern must be shaped to the needs of the total human being and the time in which he will live.

I should like to list eleven elements which I believe worthy of consideration as we look to the educational system we must have for the future. These are by no means all-inclusive, but they are enough to illustrate my point. Each element represents some change from general and current practice; some elements cover the whole educational system, public and private, elementary school through college, while others relate most specifically to higher education. I would catalog them as follows:

1. *The development of more limited and better defined objectives within educational institutions.*

Our elementary and secondary schools, as well as many of our colleges and universities, have a tendency to try to be all things to all people. Part of this tendency is caused by inadequate scrutiny of the limitations of functions which any single institution can be expected to perform; part is caused by external pressures demanding curricula, courses, or activities in whatever any particular group happens to think desirable. It is out of such pressures that the tremendous proliferation of courses now so prevalent in higher education and the wide variety of activities making up the pattern of elementary and secondary schools inevitably result, with the all too frequent inclusion of courses and activities which have questionable value so far as real education is concerned.

In liberal arts colleges specifically, I question seriously the breakdown of knowledge into so many separate courses and the degree of specialization which is encouraged. In universities, I question the inclusion of training rather than educative courses in such large numbers, particularly when they sometimes degenerate into such travesties on education as techniques of fly-casting or doctoral dissertations on "A Study of School Postures and Desk Dimensions." In elementary and secondary schools, I question the desirability of attempting more than the acquisition in real depth and breadth of basic skills, knowledges, and appreciations. If the essential philosophy of our educational institutions recognizes the introductory character of formal education, then it is not necessary to scatter our energies so widely or superficially.

2. *Creation of more serious attitudes toward work and responsibility on the part of all students at all levels.*

The primary task of our institutions of learning is to teach, not to entertain. The task is also to inculcate the kinds of work habits and study habits which equip the student realistically for a world in which much will be expected of him if that world is to survive and flourish. In so doing, it is not necessary for schools and colleges to act harshly and inhumanely. It is also not necessary to equate every assignment or problem with the element of "fun," or to encourage the notion that all drudgery can be avoided and is never essential to the completion of worthwhile goals. The habits of self-discipline, of responsible action, of persistent endeavor even when the problem is intensely difficult and taxing, of careful organization and presentation of ideas—habits such as these are vital components of high quality education and can be instilled in the very young student. There is little likelihood that our colleges can aim for the highest standards of academic achievement, unless they are begun in elementary school and continued through high school. Firmness and kindliness are not incompatible, nor does rigorous academic discipline necessarily mean inflexibility and lack of regard for the individual personality.

3. *Intelligent separation of students of varying abilities with programs of study designed to tax the maximum abilities of the individual student.*

If we are committed to educating every student to the limit of his ability (and I believe we are), we cannot do so by educating them all together and in the same way. There is nothing new in this statement and many pay lip service to it, yet the fact is that we are only in the earliest stages of translating it into action. The program of advanced placement for high school students is an excellent example of a step in the right direction. We need much more of this as well as special programs and institutions which will free our colleges and universities from taking students who are patently unable to do superior academic work. The junior college is no less valuable in the total educational pattern than the four-year college or university. It has a specialized service to perform for literally millions of young people. It should be a part of the educational system everywhere, not just in a few states. That part of the President's program which provides for aptitude testing beginning at the junior high school level would have more validity if it were accompanied by a plan to create institutions of learning to take care of those students who were found unqualified for the rigors of the four-year college. Otherwise, it brings into being a program of rejection, not of maximum encouragement.

In our colleges we need to search, similarly, for the means whereby the abler student is challenged to the utmost. This holds true in both private and public institutions. All students cannot achieve an equal amount, but all can work to the limits of their capacity. If we believe in the intellectual integrity of our institutions, there is no place for sentiment as we judge the charming ne'er-do-well or the student who is merely adroit rather than academically competent. Our efforts to build the mature individual (or what Antioch College so frequently calls the "symmetrical" individual) must be predicated on the assurance that he has a right to his opportunity because he is intellectually qualified. The function of a college as a social agency, if it chooses to undertake it, *follows* and does not precede in importance its function as an agency for the pursuit of truth and the development of wisdom.

4. *Assurance of basic scientific and humanistic knowledge for all students.*

We stand today staring into outer space with a feeling of expectancy and apprehension. A universe which was hitherto remote and aloof now beckons us to draw near and at the same time repels us by its infinite magnitude. The millions of miles which gave us a sense of safety and which seemed impossible to traverse are now only an item in the space engineer's calculations. Most of us know little or nothing of what awaits us in this new outreach of man's scientific achievement. This much we *do* know: that the exploration of outer space is inevitable and comparatively close at hand; that our world will never again have its old narrow dimensions; that we must adjust ourselves to new conceptions of man's survival and growth, and in so doing must become knowledgeable in areas previously unprobed. The youth of today will live as adults in a world where interplanetary exploration and communication will have major influences on their thought and actions.

Under such circumstances it behooves us to make available through the normal educational channels a basic minimum of scientific knowledge to all. All of us must understand and learn to live with this new dimension of human achievement. The astronomical, the geophysical, the atomic, the solar, even the merely technological aspects of human research are now suddenly important, not only to the theoretical scientific scholar, but to the average man and women. The educational system we develop must offer such knowledge to all in simple understandable terms. From elementary school on, this knowledge must be disseminated steadily and accurately.

Coupled with this new and pressing necessity is that of preserving and nurturing a deep respect for and a recognition of the essential values in humanistic culture. Knowledge of the scientific world will help us to survive, but adherence to the values taught by the humanities will keep us free men. We cannot relax for a moment our efforts to show by our educational actions our conviction that the liberalizing arts are still the mainstay and hope for freedom and peace. Higher education has the heaviest part of this burden to carry, but the secondary schools and the less formal adult education efforts in this country have a share also. Scientific knowledge and humane understanding are corollary necessities for modern democracy, not just for its leaders, but for all its citizens.

5. *More extensive and continuous use of educational facilities.*

As part of the necessity I mentioned earlier for more serious purpose and rigorous study in our schools and colleges, the way in which we are using presently available facilities needs to be carefully examined. There is no question about the need for new building construction at all levels, and indeed another disappointment in the President's proposal is its failure even to make a gesture in this direction. But parallel to this need is one of making certain that we are using what we now have to capacity. I would say that too many of our facilities stand idle too much of the time and are actually closed for months at a stretch. The old tradition of closing schools in May or June so that the boys can work on the farms persists, even though the purpose has long since disappeared in most places. I would say, also, that in many schools longer days would be advantageous, affording opportunities for longer class periods and providing some counter-balance to the time used now for peripheral activities which all too frequently make concentrated work almost an impossibility. Of course, there is little point in providing new facilities or scheduling more use of present ones if there are no teachers to man them, but that is a topic in itself.

6. *Continuing exploration and use of special devices such as teaching aids, with thorough understanding of their limitations.*

I suppose there must have been those in the fifteenth century who sturdily maintained that Caxton's printing press and its successors should be ignored and that we should keep to our illuminated manuscripts. So today there are those who refuse to recognize that the mass media of communication as presently developed have tremendous potential value for education. Experiment after experiment proves the value of films, of radio, of television (to mention the most common) for performing certain educational tasks economically and effectively. Yet, the regular bugaboo continues to be raised that this is an insidious way of replacing the teacher and that the quality of education is bound to be lowered by the use of these media. The fact is that specific training can be given, and factual elements of education can be taught, in most cases just as effectively by the new means and in some cases more effectively. Used as a teaching aid, as a tool in the hands of the teacher, any of these media can serve us well. It is only as a limited tool that they are intended to serve, a tool which frees teachers of hours of work because of the numbers who can be reached at the same time and which on occasion can put the student in contact with truly great teaching. Only the fanatics would claim more for the use of the mass media.

We must train teachers to use these media wisely and students to appreciate their value. Perhaps, in the process, we may even be able ultimately to develop enough appreciation on the part of both so that the proportion of hours now devoted to complete drivel in television, for example, will be materially cut down because they will be rejected by an audience with a sense of discrimination and taste.

7. *Expansion and deepening of modern language programs.* If we believe in world intercommunication as a basis for peaceful solution of our problems, we should recognize the necessity for being able to communicate in languages other than our own. Our attitude very largely has been that if the rest of the world wishes to talk with us, let them talk in English. Most of our tourists apparently take such an attitude. With travel to all parts of the world becoming so rapid and so commonplace, there is no question of our citizens being in regular contact with those of other countries, either for business, education, or pleasure. Our insistence upon English as *the* language is just one more psychological hurdle we have set up for the other cultures to jump over in order to learn to understand us. For, rightly or wrongly, they interpret our unwillingness to speak to them occasionally in their own tongues as a gesture of superiority on our part. And they resent this gesture deeply.

We need, therefore, to re-examine the extent to which we now encourage the study of foreign languages, the specific languages we are offering, and the particular patterns of instruction. There seems to be an enormous mass of documentary evidence, for example, to prove that very young children can be introduced to a new language much more easily and effectively than in their high school or college years. Yet we start our foreign language instruction in high school, and even then the student may ignore it if he chooses although he may be a prospective candidate for college. Are we offering instruction in the *right* languages, right in the sense that they have meaning and worth for the world of today and tomorrow? Are we presenting language instruction in such a manner as to open up new cultural vistas and to bridge the gaps in understanding? It seems to me that we should be concerned about these and similar questions.

8. *New emphasis upon the study of non-Western cultures.*

One needs to take only a glance at the newspapers day after day to realize how many of the world's problems are centered in non-Western areas and how much we in America are involved, willingly or unwillingly, in the solution of these problems. One needs to take only a similar glance at the curricula of our educational institutions to realize that only the most limited attention is ordinarily given to the study of non-Western cultures. Our procrastination in learning something about the Russian people and their background (to say nothing of their language) is bad enough; to continue such procrastination in regard to India, the Middle East, the Near East, or China is even worse. We are deeply distressed about the progress of Russia, but not distressed enough to make it mandatory that every student be taught how and why such progress has taken place. Some of us see already that the future struggle in the world will be with the brand of communism now flourishing in China, rather than the Russian variety. Yet what do we teach in our schools today about China, new or old? As a matter of fact, we recently developed an attitude toward learning in this country which classified—in the minds of many people—any exploration of political, social, or philosophical ideas other than our own Western brand as tantamount to subversive action. The battle to change this attitude is not yet completely won.

We must begin to give the non-Western cultures a new and more favored place in our curricula, even if this means eliminating or cutting down some of our present preoccupations. We need to start with the development of a new respect for and understanding of the heritage of knowledge and wisdom these cultures offer the world and follow this with increased attention to their contemporary ideas and actions, political, economic, and social.

9. *Revision of curricula in teacher-training institutions to meet the necessities of the time.*

Since so many of our teachers, particularly in elementary and secondary schools, are products of teacher-training institutions, any effort to upgrade our educational process should inevitably involve an examination of what is currently being taught them to complete their background and training. Such matters as the extent of subject matter content and humanistic learning in the total curriculum, the validity of present certification requirements, the ability of teacher trainees to comprehend and utilize modern aids to the teaching process, and the degree of attention given to the personal leadership qualities of prospective teachers are typical of the kind of analysis necessary. Perhaps a good starting point might be a nation-wide study of current curricula and practices carried out by a disinterested agency or committee. An investment of funds for such a study by foundations and the federal government would have tremendous effect in terms of the immediate and long-range recommendations which could be expected. A pattern for action could thus be drawn which would go far in focussing national attention on this key aspect of our development of teacher resources.

10. *Broad expansion of continuing education of a liberalizing type.*

Not only does the formal educational system of America need re-evaluation, but that more amorphous and steadily growing segment which embraces adult education of many types needs encouragement, particularly in those aspects which liberalize and broaden the mind. A by-product of such encouragement would be a growing realization by our citizenry of the key importance of education generally. Another by-product would be increased communication among educational institutions and agencies of all types. The major result, however, would be the development of a new personal attitude by men and women at all levels of educational experience as they continued their own participation in an on-going learning process. Leadership for the encouragement of such continuing education must come to a large extent from the established and permanent institutions of learning.

11. *Systematic development of co-operative teaching and facility arrangements among schools and colleges.*

A careful look at present educational practices in our schools and colleges reveals two facts: first, that not enough is known by one institution of what another is doing successfully; and second, that in each institution's efforts to provide a maximum program of studies and facilities to undergird these studies a great deal of unnecessary duplication is taking place. Let me use the fairly small liberal arts colleges with modest resources as an illustration of my points. Each is doing things which have educational significance generally, but normally very little is known of what the other is doing. In fact, sometimes a kind of professional pride develops bordering on jealousy which guards achievements lest others benefit from doing the same things successfully. Also, each tries, in spite of the limitations of resources, to offer to students as much of the total spectrum of knowledge as possible, and in the process each frequently spreads itself rather thin. There are serious gaps in all programs, yet too many hold tenaciously and almost grandly to a position of isolation.

With modern communications and transportation at such a high state of development, I fail to see why a number of institutions, even some distance geographically from each other, cannot band together to offer as a group the total curricular plan for an area of knowledge. Faculty members from each of the institutions could develop specific portions of such a broad plan and by a carefully integrated program of exchange teaching could bring to the students of all the institutions involved the opportunity to study whatever aspects seemed desirable during the course of a total college career. Library and other facilities could similarly be created co-operatively and with a minimum of duplication.

For example, each cannot offer all the foreign languages students would like to have available. Resources simply will not make this feasible. But several institutions together could provide such instruction easily, each one shouldering its share of the responsibility, each one contributing, and all sharing in the benefits. A teacher of Russian or of some Asiatic language could offer his courses on several campuses at different times. The amount of dislocation of any one teacher in this process would not necessarily be very great in terms of the amount of his travel. In fact, he might even find added stimulation and satisfaction out of his contacts with other student bodies and faculties.

I mentioned earlier the need for putting new emphasis upon the study of non-Western cultures. Here is another example of how co-operative action might help to fulfill such a need. This is a tremendously large area of knowledge to encompass, but several institutions jointly could create a program available to all through proper planning and administration.

What I am proposing will not be easy to create, especially on the college level, for all sorts of objections will be raised, some of them valid and others merely indicative of a reluctance to change traditional patterns. I can foresee the long and arduous consultation between institutional faculties which would precede the launching of such a plan of action. I can foresee the suspicion and chauvinism and academic objections which would have to be eliminated. I am none the less convinced that this kind of co-operation is possible. I am even more convinced that it is necessary and desirable. For if the private liberal arts colleges of this country believe, as they so firmly and frequently state, in the nurture of the highest quality in education, if they believe in the preservation and growth of this kind of institution, then they must learn to share each other's strengths and bolster one another's weaknesses.

There are not so many as a double handful of colleges in this country capable because of their resources of going it alone during the next twenty-five years. Colleges can survive and grow in strength by intelligent interaction, or many of them will ultimately perish separately as offerings become steadily more inadequate. I do not point this out to be dramatic or sound the voice of doom; I say it because I believe it is the simple truth.

V

I have given no more than the broadest and sketchiest kind of statement on these eleven elements of education for the future. Undoubtedly there are more elements to be considered, and even the ones I have listed need much more complete treatment. What I have discussed is sufficient, I hope, to establish my original point, namely, that the American people must look seriously to the reshaping of their patterns of education. They must look squarely and candidly at what they now have, and in full recognition of the extraordinary achievements of the past and the dedication of laymen and educators alike to bringing about such achievements, they must now move boldly into the most exciting, the most demanding, and the most promising future the world has ever known. All the changes which this future portends are paradoxically part of a steadfast and unchanging view which we as Americans still champion. We still believe that our supreme function and the purpose of our sacrifice as citizens is to develop free men in a free society. In fulfilling that function and making that sacrifice we offer to our children, and to posterity generally, the preservation of the most priceless and timeless attribute which education has to give—the self-disciplined, the broad, the untrammeled, the inquisitive mind.

9

To Be Educated Is To Be Humane

Wisdom is not necessarily a concomitant of the acquisition of knowledge, even knowledge about the highly vaunted humanities and liberal arts. Narrow-mindedness and immaturity and selfishness can be the results of a liberal arts education just as easily as magnanimity and selflessness, possibly more easily. The key lies in two essentials for the acquiring of wisdom once subject matter has been mastered: first, the personality of the teacher; and second, the relationship or relevancy of what is learned to the basic laws of life.

One necessary experience on the pathway to a mature felicity and to a full-grown individuality is full acknowledgement of our utterable and unutterable dependence upon nature and all that it contains, and upon each other.

It is my hope that the educational philosophy and the curricular approaches that will emerge from the present controversy will incorporate the best of the extremes now being offered and will not only liberate the mind of man, but also broaden and deepen his sense of humanity and humility. From absorption with self he will move upward to absorption with selflessness, thus affording some measure of promise that the world of the future will be a better and more peaceful world.

(Address at an Antioch College Assembly, June 3, 1958)

I

IT HAS BEEN A FASCINATING EXPERIENCE TO LISTEN TO THE MANY and varied voices all crying out over American education in the new perspective of a nuclear and space age. The cacophony of sound has ranged from the shrill tones of invective and accusation to the deep intonations of impending doom intermingled with calm baritone notes telling us to take heart, that all is well, and that there is nothing to fear. No blending or harmony has been possible as yet, but as we are surrounded again and again with rising or falling reverberations, the mood of calm complacency seems to dominate the music more and more. It is my guess that soon the earlier and more strident recitatives will become a somnolent lullaby, allowing education and educators to sleep quietly once more, happily pillowed on their traditional and unchanged curricula.

There were several stages in the reactions to the Sputniks. At first, the American public was upset and angry and so were the educators. Then followed the period during which everyone agreed something was wrong and scrambled mightily to find some person or group on which to hang the blame. Government quickly shifted its scapegoat role to the scientists who laid the fault neatly and squarely on the shoulders of education as a whole before the educators quite grasped what was being done to them. Once aware, however, the educators (after first making some menacing gestures to the American parent and murmuring something about teaching what the public insisted upon having taught) discovered that their best defense was an offense. They insisted suddenly upon the rightness and efficacy of what they had been doing. They trotted out achievement statistics by the ream and militantly invoked the names of Terman, Binet, and Rorschach. Time and circumstance smiled upon them, for just as they seemed pinned against the wall, America started frantically lobbing satellites into outer space until it had accumulated a batting average respectable enough to warrant its membership in the major leagues. This was the signal for almost everyone to relax again, for now we knew once more we were better than the Russians, our national pride was re-bolstered, and we could afford to go back to our normal anti-intellectual state and start worrying about the recession. After the action came the reaction, and, like Dr. Pangloss, we were again living in the best of all possible worlds. It was time to stop being foolish and sentimental about such things as school bond issues and get busy with "You Auto Buy" campaigns.

To say that there was no residue of good from all the events that ensued would be inaccurate. Much good did come, although it is too early to tell whether or not the benefits will be permanent. Temporarily, at least, the American people were shocked to discover how shabbily they had been treating their teachers and intellectuals in general. The citizenry were led to look more closely and analytically at what goes on today in the name of education. Bills were introduced into Congress, where many of them will remain. Some will emerge as law even though they may be mild in their effectiveness. And some people will go on thinking and wondering, particularly some educators who had grave doubts before and have even greater ones now.

Some echoes of all the noise that started late in 1957 are still ringing in my ears, or perhaps I am hearing things that actually were never said. I would certainly prefer to believe that *some* of them were never said, but I am afraid they were. For example, there was the request that two prominent educators made to high school principals all over the country urging them to boycott a national magazine that dared to attack present educational philosophies. Here was academic freedom in reverse by its most ardent champions. Out of all the numbness that can result from having one's ears assaulted so loudly and so often, I have emerged with a reasonably clear notion of what most of the shouting was about.

II

Two basic and extreme philosophies of education seem to have ranged themselves counter to one another during the controversy. One of these has been labelled the "life adjustment" or "progressive education" philosophy and has been so castigated in the public press that today it hangs around the necks of some educators like an albatross. John Dewey is the villain of the piece and his works are likened to a species of marijuana leading only to exhilaration and disaster. Laymen by the dozen, with one eye on the shortcomings of their children and the other on the best-selling possibilities of their utterances, have rushed into print to extol the splendid days of their own youth with its educational excellence, while at the same time reviling the modern curriculum and teaching methods.

In opposition to the "life adjustment" view the virtues of the Little Red Schoolhouse with its Spartan simplicity have been brought out of retirement, dusted off, and presented once more. The good, solid, down-to-earth characteristics of early American education have been set up again as a model. The *intellectual* growth of the undergraduate college student, or even the secondary school student, is put forward as the only important element of this second philosophy. Concentration upon the fundamentals, strong mental discipline, and abolition of "frills" are the planks of this educational platform. The teacher training institutions with all their alleged pernicious influences have been relegated summarily to the ash heap.

It has been difficult for the "life adjustment" faction to bear up under this onslaught. The strategy has been to deny everything and stand firm. The so-called "frills" have been defended hotly, and words like "enrichment," "social consciousness," "usefulness to society," and "individual differences" have been flying through the air like unguided missiles. The advocates of the methods now generally employed have pointed out with some justification that those who are most critical of Dewey's philosophy of education have never even bothered to read his works let alone try to understand them. They have pointed proudly to the rise of literacy, the spread of education through the American population, and the achievements of the last forty years brought about by the human products of the system of education now in vogue.

One of the forgotten characteristics of this controversy is that it has a somewhat familiar look to those who are students of educational history. If one examines what has occurred in the last several decades, one realizes that the cyclical quality of American education is one of its most evident traits. Educational ideas have a way of emerging, being popular for a while, gradually falling into disuse, and then suddenly re-emerging as though they had never been thought of before. I could give example after example of this sort of circumstance. The one-room school with all the age levels together was the original pattern for elementary public school education. As education was made available to more and more young people, the schools inevitably enlarged and separated into grades. The one-room school came to be looked upon as backward and insufficient in what it provided. Yet now I read descriptions of attempts to return to the non-graded school as a psychologically superior type.

Closely allied to this example is the full circle that has been described in regard to homogeneous versus heterogeneous grouping in classes. We have gone step by step from one to the other and back again. The project method of teaching, the phonetic method of learning to read, the unit approach, the child-centered versus the subject matter-centered curriculum—there are many such illustrations. I have always remembered the comment I heard in my first year of teaching from an elderly, white-haired lady of more than fifty years of teaching experience, who said with a shrug of her shoulders, "I've watched them come and I've watched them go. Nothing ever really changes very much if you wait a while."

If you think, perchance, that the present complaints about the softness of modern education are a new and strange phenomenon, listen to this quotation:

> When we were boys, boys had to do a little work in school. They were not coaxed; they were hammered. Spelling, writing and arithmetic were not electives and you had to learn.
>
> In these more fortunate times, elementary education has become in many places a sort of vaudeville show. The child must be kept amused and learns what he pleases. Many teachers scorn the old-fashioned rudiments; and it seems to be regarded as a misfortune and a crime for a child to learn to read and spell by the old methods. As a result of all the improvements, there is a race of gifted pupils more or less ignorant of the once-prized elements of an ordinary education.

The statement sounds as though it were made by one of our very modern critics. It is actually a quotation from the New York *Sun*, printed on October 5, 1902, and reprinted in *Harper's* magazine in May of 1958.

What also seems to have been forgotten in this recent tussle, during which tempers have grown short and feelings have run high, is that there is a middle ground where agreement may be reached. If there has been an extreme adherence to the "life adjustment" philosophy, there is now an equally dangerous possibility that we shall swing to a similarly extreme concentration upon intellectual growth to the exclusion of everything else. Out of a laudable and entirely justified desire to strengthen and deepen the quality of teaching and to insist more forthrightly upon the discipline which real learning imposes has frequently come a reckless attack on all the other aspects of education which help to create a personality and an individual.

There is not the slightest reason to believe that complete concentration on the intellect will develop the kind of creativity, the sense of personal responsibility, or the maturity for which everyone seems to be pleading. It will not occur as an accidental by-product. Wisdom is not necessarily a concomitant of the acquisition of knowledge, even knowledge about the highly vaunted humanities and liberal arts. Narrow-mindedness and immaturity and selfishness can be the results of a liberal arts education just as easily as magnanimity and selflessness, possibly more easily. The key lies in two essentials for the acquiring of wisdom once subject matter has been mastered: first, the personality of the teacher, and second, the relationship or relevancy of what is learned to the basic laws of life.

I hesitate to belabor the point about the importance of the teacher, and yet it is impossible to discuss the problems of education without doing so. We are presently engaged in the most absorbing and promising experiments designed to find new methods of teaching. We are discovering the possibilities of television, of other visual and aural aids, of electronic machines, of student assistants, of independent study, of language laboratories, and a host of other departures from the traditional and conventional. Some of these experiments will prove effective enough to make significant changes in educational practices of the future. When we come to the attainment of wisdom, however, we are faced with a problem that no mechanical device or ingenious shuffling of time and facilities can solve for us. We are faced with the simple fact that wisdom is rarely attained except through the interaction and counterstimulation of personalities: the personality of the student who stimulates the teacher to his best efforts by showing intellectual curiosity and an inordinate desire to find his place in the world; the personality of the teacher, reacting to this welcome pressure from the student and possessing a breadth of mental outreach that opens the student's eyes to his true purpose for being.

The component of wisdom as the goal of education, therefore, transcends such things as subject matter and is rather the distillation of the teacher's experience, his values, his awareness of man in his most humanitarian aspects, his compassion for man's weaknesses, his zeal to assist in the correction of the world's tragic blunders and the amelioration of its illnesses. It is the *person* whom we ultimately remember as a teacher, not the subject matter of his course.

Thus, wisdom emerges out of the ability of the teacher so to shape the curriculum and to present his subject that what he offers has relevancy to life itself. The important thing to remember in this connection is that relevancy to life cannot be limited to the individual and his own needs. It is on this point that I believe the real misunderstanding exists between those who condemn Dewey's philosophy and those who think they have been following it. Too many modern educators have interpreted "life adjustment" to mean developing the individual so that he fits in easily and pleasantly with his surroundings and his peers. Following such an interpretation they have concentrated so much upon the development of the individual as to make him lose sight of the world around him so far as his own place in it for service is concerned.

As they have increased and refined their abilities to analyze scientifically the student's strengths and weaknesses, they have used their analyses to excuse his normal immature inadequacies, have shifted the blame from him to others, and have tended to encourage his selfishness and preoccupation with himself as a psychological study. In all this they have been aided and abetted by the parental attitudes of the times, the disintegration of family life as an educative force, and the tremendous pressures of materialism. The result in many instances, therefore, has been a hedonistic generation, concentrating upon its own pleasures and privileges and artfully (as well as correctly) blaming its elders for the shortcomings it displays.

If I understand Dewey correctly, his plea for linking education to usefulness in society was anything but an attack on intellectualism except when this had degenerated into mere pedantry. He was not advocating the kind of superficial and well-nigh ridiculous courses and methods which were developed by some of his so-called followers. He said:

> Education, if it is really education, should send [youth] forth with some unified sense of the kind of world in which they live, the directions in which it is moving, and the part they have to play in it. The schools should have given them some sort of intellectual and moral key to their contemporary world. . . . As for methods, the prime need of every person at present is capacity to think; the power to see problems, to relate facts to them, to use and enjoy ideas.[1]

Dewey said this more than a dozen years ago, and his own detractors are saying the same thing today as though it were in opposition to his views.

Dewey was interested in promulgating the principle of relevancy to life in its deepest sense and thereby strengthening a democratic society. Properly interpreted and translated, this principle gives education a responsibility for awakening the student to a realization of his place in the cosmos and thereby making him eager to be a participant in the total life rather than a detached observer or even a fugitive from reality. Such participation goes far beyond the stage during which the student learns about himself. Properly guided, it is far more than methodology; but somewhere along the line, educational methods became the high gods of the Deweyites, and in their preoccupation with these gods the heart of the matter was forgotten or brushed aside.

The validity of looking beyond mere intellect in fashioning men and women of the future is to me still a strong principle, able to withstand its challengers. Think of what Horace Mann, Antioch's first president, said in 1853, the year of Antioch's founding: "The more I see of our present civilization and of the only remedies for its evils, the more I dread intellectual eminence when separated from virtue." In one of his public addresses he asked whether the youth in our schools are being educated in reference to themselves and their private interests only, or with regard to the great social duties and prerogatives that await them

1. John Dewey, *Problems of Men* (New York: Philosophical Library, 1946), p. 90.

in adult life. More than a century later we are asking the same question.

The canker of materialism eating at the heart of society today is similarly gnawing at the vitals of the liberal arts college, causing it to distort itself into strange shapes and fashions and to succumb to society's pressures. Out of such distortions arise confusing intepretations of purposes and objectives, mystifying forays into vocational training and specialization, antithetical declarations of commitment to the strengthening of broad or basic values and at the same time to the encouragement of training techniques. These diversionary activities and courses often do not come about from the free will of the college, but rather from the pressures upon it to turn out products equipped to make a living whether or not they are at the same time equipped to make a life. The college diploma as the open sesame to a well-paying job is far too often the sole motivation of the parent as he sends his son or daughter to the campus.

The materialism of society today is not an expression of disregard for cultural elements of life. The very contrary is true. More people than ever before in America are absorbed in the broadest kind of diversification of leisure-time activities. According to Frederick Lewis Allen[2] and F. B. Turck,[3] between 1940 and 1950 ticket sales for the legitimate theatre and the opera went up eighty-five per cent as against only forty-two per cent for motion pictures. Attendance at serious music concerts jumped eighty-eight per cent. More dollars were spent for them in 1951 than for baseball. By 1951 there were 659 symphonic groups in the United States and the number of towns and cities having regular concert series had doubled since 1940. Sales of paintings, attendance at art museums, and the number of art museums had increased at an almost fantastic rate. The sales of art supplies were ten times as great in 1949 as in 1939. In part these changes were a reflection of economic prosperity, but only in part.

---

2. Frederick Lewis Allen, *The Big Change*, 1952.
3. F. B. Turck, "The Great American Explosion," *Scientific Monthly*, September, 1952.

No, there is evidence that America's tastes are improving, but the materialistic *attitude* toward life persists and has tremendous influence upon our educational system. Success is still measured by its visual and tangible forms rather than the degree of service to humanity. It is inevitable that this should affect our educational system, substituting the cultivation of superficial values for basic ones. This is not a reason, however, to throw out the consideration of *all* values and to concentrate on knowledge for its own sake.

The development or lack of development of individuality in youth has also had its share of attention as education has been criticized. A great cry has been that we must beware the perils of conformity, and I would agree that real dangers lie in this direction. But equally real dangers lie in the development of an incompleted or arrested kind of individuality, the kind that never gets beyond the consideration of one's self. Education can take part of the blame for this, but not all. The family can be given a share, too, in its frequent inability to establish values in early life which will withstand the tests and challenges of time. This is, after all, a primary function of family life. But it has more and more been shunted off on the educational system, which was intended to test and strengthen values, not to originate them. Too many young people arrive near the end of college life, therefore, with an interpretation of individuality that has little relevance to life outside themselves. For example, here are a few statements written by undergraduate students (I shall not name their college) in which they give some account of their philosophy of life.

> Real freedom only comes in divorcing oneself from others. In the group the individual tends to become an amalgam of many people, beliefs, wants.

> There is no philosophy worth having save that which one arrives at himself.

> The vilest thing that can happen to a person is the subjugation of his will to another person.

> I do not consider my state of happiness, real or imagined, to be in any way dependent on or related to what I think of other people or what they think of me.
>
> The only meaning that an individual can find in life is the meaning that he creates in his own separate existence.
>
> I want to touch the solid ground of unvarnished reality and sheer stark existence, instead of wasting time on the tinny superstructure of society and perhaps adding an ornament to it.
>
> The doctrine that I preach is of independence, independence from other people, places, institutions.[4]

Even when we realize that such absolutist views will give way in time, we still wonder at how little our educational system seems to have achieved for these young people in leaving them so far short of wisdom. What sorts of personalities have touched them, and with what irrelevancies have they been concerned? Henry Murray, Harvard professor of clinical psychology, has much to offer on this point. He says:

> To tell the truth, individuality as a value, as a boast, as a stead for pride, strikes me, in certain moods as naive, shallow, and pretentious. It lacks the depth dimension. As an ideal it plays a strategic role, no doubt, during those years in a young man's life when he must discover his own nature, select a vocation appropriate to his talents, and, in so doing, grow in a differentiated way out of the family husk in which he was imbedded and out of the colloidal matrix of his adolescent peer group. But, beyond that, it is too apt to lead on to illusory self-inflations, false poses, and counterfeit aggrandizements, tumors of the ego. The individualist says "I" with a special stress and accent. "*I* did this," "*I* did that," always "I," as if he had never come upon the fact that he could not do any of these things without the participation of nature and also, in most cases, of other people. It does not seem that he has ever humbly acknowledged that he is pretty nearly powerless vis-à-vis his own body and vis-à-vis the greater part of his personality and mind. He is not able to decide that the heart shall keep on beating. He is not able to decide that a plentiful supply

---

4. Henry A. Murray, "The Meaning and Content of Individuality in Contemporary America," *Daedalus*, 87, No. 2 (1958), 39.

> of energy and enthusiasm will be available next morning. He is not able to decide to fall in love. He is not able to decide that fresh and significant ideas shall spring to mind to enliven his conversation or to advance his thought. He cannot choose to choose what he will choose. From first to last he is utterly dependent for his being, for the capacity to sense, feel, think, and act, for the delight of living, upon the perfect orchestration of billions of uncontrollable, irreversible, and inscrutable goings on within him. And yet his objective knowledge of these facts does not bring him round to wisdom. He takes it all for granted: accepts it without reverence, without gratitude, and without grace. The fault, as I see it, lies in a kind of hydrocephalus of the ego. The ego shouts "I am the master of my fate!" and a minute later one tiny embolus slits the thinspun life and puts an end to all that nonsense.[5]

Murray remarks that in the past individuality was based on a "commitment to an ideal bigger than itself, whereas today it is founded on the refusal to accept the yoke of any such commitment." He goes on in a more positive vein to say that individuality is something to be built for the sake of something else. It is a structure of potential energies for expenditure in the service of an idea, a cultural endeavor, the betterment of man, an emergent value. "Individual self is made only to be lost—that is, only to pledge itself to some enterprise that is in league with a good future, and thereby find itself once more, but this time as the actor of a living myth, an instrument of culture."

The point is, therefore, that one necessary experience on the pathway to a mature felicity and to a full-grown individuality is full acknowledgment of our utterable and unutterable dependence upon nature and all that it contains, and upon each other. Acknowledgment of this in one's very marrow gives rise to wonder, awe, reverence, gratitude, and hope. Individuality emerges as an ideal only after one has acquired conscience, character, and the habits of consideration and seriousness. An educational philosophy that encourages such individuality and the creativeness it engenders is to me a proper one for America, but one that ignores this or misinterprets it can do infinite harm.

---

5. *Ibid.*, p. 41.

III

What I have been saying is that an educational system devoted single-mindedly to the acquisition of knowledge is not enough. It is insufficient to meet the needs of our time, especially in the American framework of providing education for as many as will accept it. There is danger that in fighting anti-intellectualism one can create an intellectual vacuum or at best an intellectual hot house. Just as we keep urging the scientist to be a man first and a scientist next, so we must equally urge the same for the intellectual. To be a man, the truly educated person must have a sense of the relevancy of his own existence to that of the world he inhabits. It is completely possible for an educational system to foster such a sense of relevancy with all its spiritual overtones and at the same time provide the basic discipline and the tools of knowledge so loudly championed today. Through such an amalgam of purposes can come new directions and new achievements for education.

We know that in the pattern of educational diversity we follow in America a college can be many things to many people, things good and things bad. It can be a center for sociable activity or a center for social consciousness; it can be a hunting ground for a husband, a deterrent to military service, a convenient headquarters for doing nothing; it can also be a proving ground for effective living, a setting for meditative thinking, a fountainhead of wisdom; it can be an encourager of skepticism or a bulwark of denominationalism; it can make monsters or it can make men; it can reconcile and strengthen values or it can destroy them; it can develop pseudo-individualists or it can nurture the free, creative mind mature enough to see that its freedom and creativity must inevitably be directed toward society as a whole rather than toward an inward and egoistic satisfaction.

It is my hope that the educational philosophy and the curricular approaches that will emerge from the present controversy will incorporate the best of the extremes now being offered and will not only liberate the mind of man, but also broaden and deepen his sense of humanity and humility. From absorption with self he will move upward to absorption with selflessness, thus affording some measure of promise that the world of the future will be a better and more peaceful world.

10

Quality in Education

The whole nation appears to be alert these days, in what I hope is a more than transitory fashion, to the need for quality in American education. The pursuit of excellence has come into its own on a new and broader scale.... Quality in education should always have been our goals; we needed no Sputniks to tell us that.

⁊ ⁊ ⁊

The American dream of equality of opportunity does not encompass making everyone the same in station and degree of success, nor does it have as its intention the education of everyone in the same degree and in the same way. What it does encompass and intend is the opportunity for everyone to be educated to the limit of his ability. The limit of that ability is to be determined, not by birth or by social status or even by artificial means of screening early in life, but rather by the individual capacity of the person as evidenced by his continuing achievement and the growing strength of his motivation.

⁊ ⁊ ⁊

An educational system is no broader, no deeper, no more humane, no more dynamic, no more qualitative in its aspects than the people who are its architects and leaders, or those who are the students to be taught according to its doctrines. In the last analysis, the quality of education is the quality of each of us.

(From an Address at an Antioch College Assembly, December 16, 1958)

I

IT SEEMS TO ME THAT HIGHER EDUCATION GENERALLY IS INCLINED TO take itself too seriously and in the process is vulnerable to the loss of its sense of humor. We all seem to forget, for example, what a short distance we have traveled along the path of human progress and how swift has been our pace. A statement by Lieutenant General S. E. Anderson, commander of the Air Research and Development Command, illustrates this point well:

> In his book, *A Guide to Earth History*, Richard Carrington put it this way. "If we imagine the whole of earth's history compressed into a single year, then on this scale, the first eight months of the year would be completely without life. The following two months would see only the most primitive of creatures, ranging from viruses and single-celled bacteria to jellyfish, while mammals would not have appeared until the second week in December. Man, as we know him, would have come onto the stage at about 11:45 p.m. on December 31. The age of written history would have occupied little more than the last 60 seconds of the clock."
>
> Expanding this condensed time cycle a bit, Mr. J. Lewis Powell of the Office of the Assistant Secretary of Defense for Supply and Logistics illustrates the phenomenal rate of progress in another way. He relates it to the years lived by some of us in this room—give or take a few—about fifty years. Reduced to fifty years, this would mean that ten years ago man stopped living in caves; five years ago someone invented picture writing; two years ago Christianity was started; five months ago, the printing press was invented; ten days ago, electricity was discovered; yesterday the Wright Brothers flew the first plane; TV was invented since this meeting started; jets came into being since I stood up to speak. Please note that on this basis almost everything that makes up our material world, from inside plumbing to jets and missiles, would have been invented within the last 24 hours.

My purpose in emphasizing the need for perspective is to plead for less pessimism as one considers the problems still remaining to be solved. We have made and are making real progress, whether it be in the strengthening of the campus, in the amelioration of social injustices locally or nationally, or in our efforts to improve the quality of higher education in this country. We need to remember that progress on ideas that really count is at best a halting, stumbling thing. But it stumbles forward, and therein lies our hope.

I doubt that we are all fully aware of the paradoxical character of our progress on this earth. First of all, there is the paradox of an expanding population and a shrinking world, not physically shrinking but shrinking because of the tremendous strides made in increasing communication and mobility. With news flashed around the world in a matter of seconds, with two-hour jet flights from New York to London or Paris expected within five years, with almost every citizen of our country provided with the rapid and inexpensive means to propel himself physically somewhere else, our world is contracting around us dramatically and inexorably. This contraction produces another paradox. Instead of our progress contributing to a spirit of freedom of understanding or of well-being as we reap the benefits of our scientific devices for communications, travel, and interaction, it has actually accentuated our fears and anxieties, has decreased our trust in one another, and has done little to lessen the world's aches and pains. To carry this paradox still further, it would appear that the more we have been able to increase our contacts with parts of the world hitherto comparatively unknown (at least unknown to us) the less we seem to have achieved a firm grasp of the position of leadership which is our lot. It is small wonder that under such circumstances we are not fulfilling our role adequately, and we wear the mantle of world responsibility like a hair shirt.

Then, too, there is the paradox of a world with widely different cultures rooted in almost ageless philosophy and at the same time a world which, in total, is experiencing the impact of a modern industrial and scientific revolution. The long-accepted ideas and ideologies which make people different are competing with the impact of contemporary material things which are tending to make people become the same the world over. The inscrutable Oriental shrine is being shouldered by the frank skyscraper; the exotic bazaars of the Middle and Near East lie cheek by jowl with the movie palaces and modern department stores. The African veldt resounds to the roar of the auto and airplane motor or the crack of the high-powered rifle as much as to the beat of the tom-tom or the whiz of the arrow. The Polynesian is beginning to know the efficacy of canned foods as well as his native poi and breadfruit.

If all the world is to become kin, is it to be through a meeting of inquiring minds and a fusing of free spirits, or through the sharing of experiences with refrigerators, inside plumbing, motion pictures, motor cars, and tractors? Will the latter actually pave the way for better understanding, or will they merely increase the number of people preoccupied with a higher material standard of living? Is there danger that the spread of a higher material standard of living can debase the human character just as readily as it can elevate it?

I say all this because there is such danger of forgetting the simple basic truths inherent to the betterment of the world, and therefore inherent to the development of new and broader objectives in education. It is a fundamental truth, for example, that in the encouragement and nurture of the educational process for everyone lies the ultimate hope for solution of the world's problems. But this educational process must be of a certain sort, must have certain components, if it is to justify our hopes.

II

The whole nation appears to be alert these days, in what I hope is a more than transitory fashion, to the need for quality in American education. The pursuit of excellence has come into its own on a new and broader scale. As we look ahead, we can only pray that this pursuit will not have to be stimulated by the degree of success the Soviet Union achieves periodically in science or in anything else. Quality in education should always have been our goal; we needed no Sputniks to tell us that. It will be a sad day for us if the only way we can become awakened to the importance of quality in education is by meeting the challenge of every Soviet-manufactured crisis. The future of America rests on more positive and enduring approaches, I am sure.

Thornton Wilder, in his wonderful play, *Our Town*, says, "Every time a child is born into the world it's Nature's attempt to make a perfect human being. Well, we've seen Nature pushing and contriving for some time now. We all know she's interested in quantity; but I think she's interested in quality, too."

What do we mean by quality? What do we mean specifically by quality in education? What do we mean even more specifically by quality in American education as a means to assure or guarantee the equal opportunity we have set as the goal for every man, woman, and child in our country? It seems to me that we need to have answers to these questions. Strangely enough, with all the talk and the writing of the last hundred and fifty years about American education, its primary objective of equal opportunity still is misunderstood by millions of citizens including more than a few eminent educators. There seems to be no way to define the objective often and recurrently enough, clear as it may be, to make sure everyone understands and agrees. At the risk of being elementary in my approach, let me state the case once more.

The American dream of equality of opportunity does not encompass making everyone the same in station and degree of success, nor does it have as its intention the education of everyone in the same degree and in the same way. What it *does* encompass and intend is the opportunity for everyone to be educated to the limit of his ability. The limit of that ability is to be determined, not by birth or by social status or even by artificial means of screening early in life, but rather by the individual capacity of the person as evidenced by his continuing achievement and the growing strength of his motivation.

My reason for making this fundamental objective so explicit is that it is the basis upon which we must define quality in education. Here in this country, there are and there should be great diversities and differences among our educational institutions. There are and there should be large complex universities and small, relatively simply organized colleges; there are and there should be co-educational and non-coeducational institutions, denominational and non-denominational, privately endowed and publicly supported, municipal and state, technical and vocational institutes as well as institutes dedicated to the fine arts, public and private junior colleges, public and private secondary schools, and so on and on. The millions upon millions we try to educate demand and require this diversity and we must provide it to them.

But the unifying element is that of *quality*, for no part of this diverse system can countenance shoddiness in its philosophy, its program, or its personnel. Nowhere on the scale from kindergarten to the most advanced study is there a place for inferior preparation. The artisan and artist alike must be nurtured in the same tradition of high quality. It is thus that we insure the closest possible approach to the American dream of educating everyone to his utmost capacity.

There are many elements that are necessary for quality in education, some more obvious than others. Without more than mention, here are the obvious ones. The first step toward high quality is taken, for example, when a program is developed according to very carefully formulated and clearly stated objectives. Another step is the insistence upon high standards of work. Another is the acquisition and development of proper faculty. A fourth condition for quality is regular and intensive research in the techniques of instruction.

The element I should like to emphasize now, however, so necessary to high quality in education, is a new and intense awareness on the part of the student of the place of man as a free individual in a free society with personal responsibilities to that free society and to the world generally. This awareness must be inherent in every educational program designed for the student and should be a continuing thread or an undergirding foundation for everything else to be undertaken. It seems to me that there are five aspects to such an awareness, aspects that are requisites for the student's approach to the whole process of education.

The first aspect is *a desire to learn and to know.* Man is by nature an inquiring being, yet all too often our educational system seems to work counter to this tendency in him. Administrators of the formal segments of education, in their passion for orderliness and their misconception of the democratic concept of equality, have many times negated the possibility of curiosity and creativeness in the young mind. The desire to know seems to have been effectively stifled except in rare cases. Furthermore, the discipline of intellectual labor is far too infrequently applied and emphasized. All this combines to form a major stumbling block in the way of educational quality; for unless there is a predilection for learning on the part of the student, there is little likelihood of his attaining high quality work.

The stresses caused by the increasing numbers of students may well be a boon to higher education, since they may transfer out of the schools some of their present responsibilities. It is not necessarily fantastic to suppose that in the next fifty years new approaches to education will be developed making much fuller use of the home, involving community participation through libraries and other agencies, and calling upon business and industry in a direct training role. The current restiveness about the high degree of specialization in our secondary and undergraduate programs, for example, may lead to turning over gradually the whole area of vocational training to business, industry, labor, and social agencies. This would tend to free the secondary schools and colleges more and more for education of a broad and liberating nature. I do not predict this, but I think there is good likelihood of a movement in this direction. Personally, I would welcome it, but only if at the same time higher education would devote more and more of its energies to the general encouragement of learning.

Creation and nurture of a desire to learn and to know must begin, however, long before higher education comes upon the scene. They must come from the development of new teaching techniques used from the primary grades onward, techniques that tend to stimulate and foster the inquiring mind and that instill in youth the conception of the unfinished and continuing nature of their educational experience. Once such techniques have been found and proved, they must replace a good portion of those which are currently the mode in secondary schools and colleges. This is a tremendous order to fill, but no more tremendous than other orders we have filled when emergencies demanded.

I cannot overemphasize how strongly I feel about the importance of the principle of continuing education. My advocacy of this principle is founded upon my belief that instilling the desire to learn is basic and preliminary to all else that education hopes to do.

The second aspect of student awareness is that of *a sense of the future*. One of the great curses of education is its inveterate tendency to move into the future with its back turned. It stares resolutely at what is past as it fashions its plans and methods to meet tomorrow's problems. The result is that we never seem to be quite where we should be. Just as we are well on our way to the solution of yesterday's problem, today's is suddenly upon us; and while we consider how to start again, tomorrow's problem is already on the horizon. The invention of the printing press was a nasty jolt, but in time we adjusted ourselves. We even developed the lecture method when books were extremely difficult for everyone to obtain. We are still using it as a major teaching technique in spite of inexpensive mass printing, and we are still trying to make refinements of it. Radio, television, films, and other annoying gadgets came along, and now we are completely confused. Our traditions pull us in one direction, our common sense in another. And always we lag behind, doggedly solving yesterday's difficulties.

This essential conservatism has communicated itself rather strongly to students and can have the effect of making them unwilling to look steadily into the future in terms of the new kinds of knowledge they require and the new means for acquiring it. The cultivation of a sense of the future leads to a realization that education uses the past as a means for looking ahead, a process that makes of the important elements of our history a distillation of the eternal verities, a distillation that gives strength and meaning to progress. The principles of the good and magnanimous life remain the same over the ages, but only as they are applied to the new and comparatively uncharted world of the future can they offer hope.

A third aspect of the awareness a student needs is that of *the recognition of change*. It is closely linked with a sense of the future, but it is something more. It presupposes a willingness to accept the fact that the world does change, sometimes unreasonably and unpredictably, but inevitably and constantly. Furthermore, it calls for a disposition to recognize such change, to analyze it, and to act upon it accordingly and with only a pang of nostalgia for what is past. To use only one instance, and a poor one at that, preparing for citizenship in the United States today is not at all as it was even ten years ago. Today's American citizen must be ready for world responsibility. He must know his geography, his anthropology, his economics, his politics, not as domestic items, but as they touch every corner of the globe. Algerian uprisings, Venezuelan catcalls, industrial advances in China, satellite launching pads in Russia, weather stations on the polar cap, lack of milk for the Hottentots—all these and more are suddenly well within his orbit of influence and concern. Is modern education keeping pace with these changes, or at least pointing them out? Is the modern student cognizant of the part he must play?

Willingness to accept changes creates a liberating quality in the mind. There is no time for stodginess, no place for inaction, no opportunity for complacency. Properly viewed, the countless veerings and shiftings, the sudden breakthroughs in science or the development of untraditional directions in the arts, all the unpredictable breaks in the preconceived patterns are not matters for alarm or uncertainty. They are, rather, the most exciting ingredients of life and make it worthwhile.

As a fourth aspect of student awareness I would list *an uncompromising insistence upon thoroughness.* If there is to be quality there must be rigorous discipline, the kind of self-discipline that drives one to the ultimate of his ability. In late years there appears to have been a slackening of this kind of motive force, mainly because it has not always been able to become equated with practical values. The field of English language is as good a one as any to point to as a prime example of where this relaxed attitude has led us. Since one thinks in words, the mastery of one's own language is a basic requirement of effective thought. To achieve this mastery requires reading, a great deal of reading and of the best that has been written. It requires, similarly, a more clearly formulated speech. As Pulitzer Prize Winner Edgar Ansel Mowrer says, "Clarity of speech or writing demands mastery of meanings! Therefore, far from 'simplifying' its language further, an America that aims at better education must seek to preserve grammatical subtleties."

What passes for good speech and writing among college undergraduates today is disheartening to hear and behold. This casualness with the English language can easily become a habit in other studies as well. Eventually all desire to be thorough, to be precise, to be clear and logical is lost. Regardless of what particular philosophy of education one decides to espouse, thoroughness and self-discipline can be ignored only at the risk of emasculating the whole educational process.

The final aspect of student awareness is that leading to an understanding of and a dedication to *the concept of equality of opportunity*, which I described earlier. It is an all-enveloping aspect of education, surrounding the others and giving force and motivation to them. It is very personal and differs for every man. But as the American student recognizes his own potential and the opportunity democracy affords him to reach that potential, so he must be equally aware of how precious is this same concept for his fellow men all over the world. He cannot ignore moral imperatives while dealing with practical pressures. The desperate needs of mankind must reach his heart as well as his mind.

America is singularly fitted by history, by temperament, by largeness of heart to be the major champion of this concept as well as its expositor. Even with its fumblings, its errors, and its shortcomings, it has come closer to equality of opportunity than any other civilization. The Greeks in all their glory could not bring themselves to accept a society which did not include the slave. The unlimited prospect of rising to a new station in life and of fulfilling one's destiny is still peculiarly the American dream, not often enough realized, still imperfect, but offering a hope not to be lightly regarded. Of all the weapons at our command to fight the battle for humankind, this is the most potent one.

Here in the awareness of the equality of opportunity for all men is our priceless, unchanging heritage, the one which offers hope to millions regardless of how weighty the difficulties may be. In a world of the future, in a world of change, it is a liberating principle that, once fully understood, captures the imagination and loyalty of every man. It fans the desire to learn, makes us bend our backs willingly to the discipline of toil, and promotes a sense of service and participation.

III

In the America of the next fifty years, with its millions and millions of students to whom education may well mean survival, the role of education will become increasingly important. If education interprets "survival" to mean offering the skills to earn a living or to better a living standard, then it will be doing its task only incompletely. I hope it will recognize that the nobler part of its role is that of creating free and independent human beings, aware of the paradoxical interplay between independence and interdependence of man and with an understanding highly enough developed to be active participants in that interplay. This is the more difficult task, as well as the more vital.

In both aspects of the task, vocational and liberating, there can be no compromise with quality. If in everything we do, experimentally or otherwise, the measuring gauge is one of quality, then ultimately we shall raise the sights and the levels of our educational endeavor. It cannot be otherwise. The integrity of character we strive for within ourselves is dependent upon the measure of our own inner quality; the integrity of the system of education we build is inevitably the result of the same kind of quality ingredient. An educational system is no broader, no deeper, no more humane, no more dynamic, no more qualitative in its aspects than the people who are its architects and leaders, or those who are the students to be taught according to its doctrines. In the last analysis, the quality of education is the quality of each of us.

11

Science Comes of Age

The part that science has to play in the future of this planet is an awesome one. But it is a part which science is coming to recognize more clearly each day as only one of the tremendous forces of life. Through such recognitions we reach toward the maturing aspects of science and also the real hope for the world, for they are guarantees that scientists of the future will be men as well as specialists, human beings as well as researchers, humble as well as confident and courageous. Today's scientists, like a few of their great predecessors in history, are already beginning to emerge with such attributes. We must do all in our power to see that this happens more and more by the very nature of the education we provide young men and women.

(Address at a meeting of the Dayton Branch, American Chemical Society, Yellow Springs, Ohio, May 13, 1958)

I

A COLLEGE PRESIDENT SHOULD STICK TO HIS LAST, BUT EVEN A college president who is a non-scientist must have given much thought to science in recent years, to its philosophical implications, to its multitude of achievements, to the promises and dangers of its future. It would have been most remiss not to do so.

I have searched where I could and read where I could to find answers to some of the questions which have so often perplexed me. I make no pretense of being an original thinker in this area, yet certain conclusions of my own have emerged from my reading and study of scientific progress. The major conclusion of all is that I believe science, after generations of growing pains, has at last come of age.

II

It is probably difficult for many of us to realize that there was a time in the history of liberal arts colleges in America when science was held in rather low regard. The classics were the core of all intellectual activity, and scientific matters were generally disdained. Dr. George Schmidt, in his eminently readable volume, *The Liberal Arts College*, points out,

> At Columbia . . . a trustee's committee reported that a literary and scientific course established in 1830 had "rolled in on a tide of public excitement," but had attracted few students and "after dragging out a feeble existence" was abolished in 1843. The low regard in which science was held at Columbia appears in another trustees' resolution, in 1862, permitting Professor Torrey, the famous naturalist, to give a

series of lectures in botany "at such hours as will not interfere with the regular studies of the undergraduates."[1]

In more general terms, Dr. Schmidt goes on to say that in the colleges laboratory instruction was "unheard of" and that except for "an occasional distinguished scholar, the scientists remained second-rate citizens and their influence in the academic world was negligible." It was virtually impossible to provide for their training. Silliman of Yale, although classically trained and studying law, was selected by President Dwight to teach natural philosophy. In preparation he attended some lectures at the University of Pennsylvania Medical School and had a few months of study in London and Edinburgh, but this was an exception to the general rule. As Schmidt says:

> Not all students were so fortunate as to have a Silliman for a professor. Most of them seem to have remembered their classes in science, if at all, as a dreary routine of untested assertions or half-baked demonstrations with ridiculously inadequate equipment. . . . A complaint at Brown was voiced by the student newspaper in 1870 when it alleged, perhaps for propaganda purposes: "A cabinet of comparative anatomy is essential to any college. . . . Every plant and animal is an expressed thought of God, and cannot be presented through the medium of a professor. Brown has one ghastly skeleton and two or three small charts, and a few promiscuous bones! Natural philosophy is also destitute of means for making the subject interesting, if it is possible to make it so. Juniors are edified with a clothes-line and a broken fiddle."[2]

After Darwin all this changed and with amazing suddenness. The old course names of natural philosophy, natural history, mental and moral philosophy were replaced by 1890 with the now familiar categories of chemistry, physics, geology, zoology, psychology, etc. In 1866, one faculty member in Kansas at the new state university taught mathematics and natural philosophy, which comprised about one-fourth of the entire curriculum.

---

1. *The Liberal Arts College* (New Jersey: Rutgers University Press, 1957), p. 66.
2. *Ibid.*, p. 52.

Thirty years later, as an eminent specialist, he dealt with only a small part of this field as "professor of entomology and organic evolution."

> Grudgingly, incredulously, the votaries of the classics saw their claims to mental discipline and precision of thought appropriated by the cocky scientists. . . . Darwin had furnished them with a rationale, and in their new laboratories they were working out dependable techniques. These laboratories were now forthcoming, for a large part of the wealth that alumni and business philanthropists were beginning to lavish on the universities was, if not needed for a football stadium, being channeled into the science departments. From Harvard to Stanford and from Michigan to Tulane the sciences were now being supported in a style to which they had not been accustomed.[3]

By its sheer growth in size and importance, therefore, and by the way it began gradually to equal and in many cases to dominate and supplant the classics and liberal arts, science showed a maturing power that has brought it to its present state. Here is at least one respect in which it has come of age.

There are more important evidences than those of quantity and emphasis, however, that indicate science has reached its majority. One of these evidences is the involvement of science so fully and completely in the daily lives of the human race, especially here in America. The practical applications of science have revolutionized our lives in terms of what we eat and drink, what we wear, what we see and hear, how we work, the houses we live in, the ways we travel—in short, every material facet of life has changed tremendously for us as a result of a scientific impact on our world. The methods of communication, of warfare, of agriculture, of manufacture—wherever we turn we are aware of an almost overwhelming scientific influence. Most of this influence has translated itself into a standard of living well nigh unbelievable a century ago and has unlocked a veritable treasure chest of wealth hitherto undreamed of.

Obviously, the spotlight cannot fall upon science so clearly

3. *Ibid.*, p. 188.

and nakedly without disclosing certain flaws and blemishes, certain weaknesses which now at last it is facing with a new sense of understanding and responsibility. The fact that science has raised to a new level the whole problem of survival of the human race has made it vulnerable to attack even when it is not to blame. America's experience in the recent past is a striking example of this.

Anyone reading newspapers and journals or listening to the oratory of the nation's spokesmen and leaders would almost certainly be led to believe that it was the dearth of scientists in this country that led to the early domination of the Sputnik field by the Russians. It appeared that we lagged in scientific knowledge, that our educational system was to blame, that we were hopelessly outclassed by the totalitarian approach. Such feelings were not expressed unanimously, but they were expressed widely. Science and education generally were selected to be the scapegoats. So far as I can discover, however, the facts of the matter in regard to science are quite different. The best summing-up of them I have seen is in an article by Dr. Ellis A. Johnson, director of the Operations Research Office of Johns Hopkins University, a scientist, engineer, and former naval officer. Writing in a magazine called *Western World*,[4] he points out with impressive documentation that the free world is well ahead of Russia in total technical resources, in basic research, in money, in manpower, and in facilities. But he makes plain, with almost devastating candor, that the Soviet had taken a lead because of our bad organization, insufficient planning, and excessive security regulations, all of which can be laid at the door of the Department of Defense. After indicating the well-known fact that in the United States a major part in military research, development, testing, production, and planning is played by private industry, Dr. Johnson says that the direct influence of civilian science and engineering within the Department of Defense and at higher echelons of the

---

4. "Why the Russians Are Ahead in Science," *Western World*, April, 1958.

government is now almost nil. It depends primarily on scientific advisory committees with no responsibility or authority. He goes on to show the time-consuming cycle of examination of contracts now required, a process which can last as long as five years. He emphasizes the drawbacks in the cost-plus-fixed-fee type of contract which have two results, exorbitant use of technicians for each development and lack of incentive to take a risk. He stresses the fact that insufficient broad long-range planning is going on in the United States or other NATO countries. Finally, Dr. Johnson describes the rigid security regulations in the United States which make it virtually impossible for research scientists to examine accounts of prior or parallel work by other industrial or military laboratories and which limit communications within the Department of Defense itself to the point where old problems are being solved repetitiously. If we fell behind, therefore, the fault was ours, not that of science.

Still another way in which science shows definite signs of coming of age is in its new realization that it must bridge the gap between itself and society. Recently, America's first Parliament of Science was convened in Washington on the initiative of the American Association for the Advancement of Science. Both scientists and nonscientists were asked to participate as representatives of the public, government, education, the press, the arts, and the humanities. Dr. Warren Weaver, vice president of the Rockefeller Foundation, said in his statement summoning the Parliament that scientists wanted to join with others in deciding how to play "a noble part" in the use of the new dimensions of power that it has discovered. Even if we grant that this Parliament failed to spell out how it expected to play such a "noble part" or that it took very mild stands on issues which should have been met forthrightly and courageously, and even if we grant that only fifteen per cent of the nonscientific delegates originally invited actually attended, still it represented a recognition of a major problem for science, one it had largely ignored. For science to understand that a solid bridge of communication must be built to link it with society at large is an encouraging sign of progress.

It is not only now and in this century that the necessity for better understanding between science and the humanities has been championed. As far back as the eighteenth century, there were those who strove to demonstrate that science and humane learning could be combined. Montesquieu and Voltaire as social philosophers tried to draw scientific parallels in their exposition of the laws by which they said man lives. In the main, however, it is in our modern day that scholars in considerable numbers are beginning to talk about what is common to the sciences and humanities rather than what is different about them.

Perhaps the events of modern times have made the scientist more sensitive to his influence upon mankind. He has seen more dramatically than ever, because of the increased power of his inventions for destruction, a moral implication in what he has been doing. In the midst of his ordinarily confident assertions that his sole duty is to explore and explore, regardless of result, a faint doubt has crept in about whether he does not have some responsibility to his fellow man. The added fact that he cannot always find himself in agreement with his fellow scientists (on such a question, for example, as whether radioactive fallout is or is not injurious to the human race) has given him pause and has made him wonder about the infallibility of his data. Suppose others were right and he turned out to be wrong? Suppose there were devastating results because of his error? Can the scientist permit himself the luxury of a conscience? I would not attempt to answer; I merely point out that such a question is beginning to be voiced more and more often. The importance of this, as I see it, is that a new sense of humility is developing in science, in some instances even a realization that some higher power may actually be directing the universe. Some scientists are beginning to think like Jules de Goncourt when he said many years ago, "We do believe that at . . . a particular stage of scientific development, the good Lord, with a flowing white beard, will arrive on earth with his chain of keys and will say to humanity, just as they do at the Art Gallery at five o'clock, 'Gentlemen, it's closing time.'" The awareness of the infinitesimal amount that has been discovered in proportion to what still remains unknown, and of the unpredictable or horrifying results which some discoveries will occasion is a humbling and sobering thought for the modern scientist. Such unpredictability in relation to human survival makes all the more essential the need for scientists the world over to be in constant communication with one another and not to be vying secretly for the privilege of being first with a new discovery. This kind of secrecy is all too often the convenient tool of political expediency and is just as often fraught with the possibility of disaster. Political involvement is a wine too heady for most scientists to drink without losing, at least in some degree, their dedication to finding and sharing the truth with all the world. They need to think carefully about what the aftermath could be if they were to become pawns of a government.

Science, in the main, seems to be coming to terms with the spiritual side of life also, possibly as it recognizes more and more that regardless of the weighty evidence of facts presented to him and the lucidity of logic displayed to him, man appears to be predominantly governed by his emotions. It does little good to explain away these emotions in newly devised scientific terms or to say that every inner thought and act of man can be plotted by the laws of one science or another. It may be possible to manufacture goodness and magnanimity and forbearance by the application of certain physical laws, but I have never known of these values of life emerging this way. When we are all through exploring ourselves and explaining ourselves, there seems to be something outside ourselves but acting upon us which is yet unexplored and unexplained. It is this something with which the scientist struggles, for it is an intangible part of man's heritage and intangibles are the bane of the scientist's existence. Sometimes the intangible expresses itself in religious feeling, which as John Tyndall said, "is as much a verity as any other part of human consciousness; and against it, on the subjective side, the waves of science beat in vain." Doubts have been raised and faiths have been shaken as perhaps never before when more and more people have chosen to interpret the laws of science as ruling out any divine presence. Yet the increasing interdependence of man seems only to intensify his efforts to come closer to the values which were accepted thousands of years ago in the Judeo-Christian tradition as necessary to a fulfilling and meaningful life. Science has become mature as it has realized that these values cannot be ignored or swept away in the total concept of man's place in the universe. The force of man's emotions as a ruling factor in his life may well be atavistic in its source, but it still must be reckoned with in the totality of life. If I were to make a prediction, it would be that during the next fifty years a whole new era of scientific knowledge will be uncovered, subjective rather than objective in its approach, probing man's emotions as well as his mind and adding a new dimension to the already vexing difficulty which science has in adjusting itself to any outside force.

III

What I have been saying thus far has been an exposition of some of the doubts and problems that beset the scientist when he considers his relationship to the rest of the world. When matters of religion and morality and national safety and personal relationships crowd in upon him, he is unhappy because they complicate the clearly structured approaches to life in which he has been reared. The fact that he is now thinking about these problems and that he sees this area of maladjustment (no matter whether he considers himself or the non-scientific world to be maladjusted) is an evidence of maturity on his part.

This brings me to another and final point about science's coming of age. It is made manifest in the overtures that science is making toward developing science courses and programs into more creative, balanced, and integrated entities. To me this is a most important sign, for in it I see encouraging possibilities for science and the liberal arts to draw together more closely. At the same time, I recognize the difficulties standing in the way of increased understanding.

I suppose there are three attitudes that must be reflected in science education of the future if we are to move toward the solution of the present dilemmas of the world. Each of them poses philosophical and practical problems, yet the development of these attitudes could be the key to unlock doors hitherto closed almost purposefully. I would not dare to suggest that there is any assurance of any of these attitudes being developed successfully, but the increase in the maturity of science offers at least a glimmer of hope. The three characteristics I would advocate, therefore, as essential to all science courses or programs are those of *humanism*, *intelligibility*, and *a recognition of mystery*.

The fact that I champion the inclusion of a humanistic approach in science is not because, as a non-scientist, I am fighting desperately for the place of the humanities and liberal arts in education. It is rather that I truly believe the scientist should be a man first and a scientist second, and that I know no better way to move him systematically toward appreciations of the beauty and truth in the world than by developing his aesthetic insights along with his scientific ones. The scientist who can analyze a flower part by part, who can effect changes in that flower by cross-pollenization or grafting and who sees only the physical change without any appreciation of the beauty of the flower or its fragrance, that scientist is only partially mature. Similarly, the scientist who is wedded to his profession to the exclusion of literature, music, art, or philosophy is living an incomplete existence. He is cutting himself off from the rich culture of centuries, never realizing that these creative thoughts and works of man are the nearest approach that we have to immortality or to eternal verities.

The great gap between the scientists and the humanists seems to be created in large measure because the two look upon truth in dissimilar fashion. Howard Mumford Jones expresses this dissimilarity as the humanist's "concept of truth as something in being" and the scientist's "as something becoming. In a loose, general sense the humanist asks: 'How did this truth come into being?' whereas the scientist asks: 'Where do we go from here?' "[5]

Efforts in higher education, particularly in scientific institutions hitherto rather oblivious to the importance of the humanities, to revise curricula by additions of departments of humanistic studies (the Massachusetts Institute of Technology is an outstanding example) offer hope that a meeting-ground may yet be found and that the scientist of the future will have a new awareness of the heritage of the past. He will relate scientific achievement more and more to the living thought of the age that produced it. By doing so his perspectives will change and his appreciations will deepen.

When we come to the second attitude, the matter of intelligibility, I must admit that the sciences are not the only offenders. To say that most people do not understand science because its language is so technical and to point out that even scientific specialists frequently do not understand each other is to state only half the fact. The other half is that the humanists are equally guilty of surrounding their work with unintelligible jargon. Furthermore, a whole new vocabulary has sprung up in the social sciences and in education generally, leaving the layman frustrated and ready to abandon his interest or curiosity in those fields. There are all kinds of snobberies in this world, and no one has yet dealt adequately with the snobbery of vocabulary when it is employed to make confusion and difficulty out of what could be directness and simplicity. But we are thinking here of science, and so I make my plea specifically for an effort toward simpler terms in science, toward plain and direct language which fosters communication of ideas and which encourages rather than dismays the neophyte. Scientific vocabularies could use a real overhauling; a scientific lexicographer with a burning zeal for simplification

---

5. "A Humanist Looks at Science," *Daedalus*, 87, No. 1 (1958), 105.

would be a boon to us all. It is important to remember that one of the reasons Darwin had such tremendous impact upon the world was that it was possible for his work to be read and understood by the layman. The same thing can be said for Freud.

Sometimes I get the feeling that the development of intellectual jargon is a divine visitation upon us to keep us from progressing too rapidly. You will remember Chapter Eleven in Genesis which tells us about the great advances human beings had made in mechanical engineering. By introducing brick and mortar construction they built a great city.

> And the Lord came down to see the city and the tower, which the children of men builded. And the Lord said, "Behold, they are one people and they have all one language; and this is what they begin to do; and now nothing will be withholden from them, which they purpose to do. Come, let us go down, and there confound their language, that they may not understand one another's speech." So the Lord scattered them abroad from thence upon the face of all the earth, and they left off building the city.

Can it be that we are now being forced to create the Babel in order that we may never build the tower or the city?

The third attitude, one which recognizes and makes allowances for the mysteries in life, is to me an all-important component of science education for the future. It is such an attitude which still makes humility and faith and magnanimity acceptable and desirable. These are metaphysical aspects of life which have withstood scientific probings up to this point. Aldous Huxley, for example, insists that "the scientific picture of the world is inadequate for the simple reason that science does not profess to deal with experience as a whole, but only with certain aspects of it in certain contexts."[6]

Georgio de Santillana, in discussing the legacy to science left by the seventeenth century, quotes Maxwell on knowledge, "It is a universal condition of the enjoyable that the mind must believe in the existence of a law and yet have a mystery to move

6. *Science, Liberty and Peace* (New York, 1946), p. 73.

in."[7] Santillana goes on to comment that "what makes the mystery 'enjoyable' is the intuition of an identity of nature between the law we discern and that of our own being." The fact that science represents the "ordering capacity for thought" provides it with something humanistic, for such capacity includes philosophical awareness and the creative and contemplative attributes. These are all necessary to the structure of science education. The creative faculty in man must be encouraged to range far beyond the equations and formulas which bind and limit his thinking. From his imaginative conjectures about life's mysteries can come new and more penetrating discoveries.

I, perhaps, am guilty of the very unintelligibility I am decrying, but in essence I am asking that the scientist enter upon his career only after he has looked into the humanistic elements of life and that he keep these elements in mind as he tends to grow more and more the specialist. I am asking that science programs be devised to make allowances both in time and emphasis for such exploration of the humanities. If, after such exploration, science chooses to reject the values which the humanities propose as desirable, then at least it will have been with full knowledge and on the basis of the most careful scrutiny.

The part that science has to play in the future of this planet is an awesome one. But it is a part which science is coming to recognize more clearly each day as only one of the tremendous forces of life. Through such recognition we reach toward the maturing aspects of science and also the real hope for the world, for they are guarantees that scientists of the future will be men as well as specialists, human beings as well as researchers, humble as well as confident and courageous. Today's scientists, like a few of their great predecessors in history, are already beginning to emerge with such attributes. We must do all in our power to see that this happens more and more by the very nature of the education we provide young men and women.

---

7. "The Seventeenth-Century Legacy," *Daedalus*, 87, No. 1 (1958), 51.

This quotation from the introduction to a volume of *Proceedings* of the American Academy of Arts and Sciences points a way for us:

> As David McCord reminded us not long ago, the ancient figure of Daedalus himself has always been strangely modern, standing at the intersection of old dreams and new nightmares. He is remembered for his cunning, for the invention of devices no one else could duplicate or even understand. He mastered knowledge of the natural order, of technological possibilities, of magic itself. Today, this combination reappears in the popular conception of the scientists. And the same image contains a second confusion no less dangerous—that a true synthesis of the sciences and arts can still be achieved at the highest level within the individual. . . . There may be real hope for reaching a common understanding, but not by the imposition of a new system from without to replace the unified world systems we have lost. Rather, the way to the goal is precisely through discussions (between scientists and non-scientists). As Robert Oppenheimer says, "We ourselves, and with each other by our converse, can create, not an architecture of global scope, but an immense, intricate network of intimacy, illumination, and understanding."[8]

---

8. *Daedalus*, 87, No. 1 (1958), 4.

12

Education for a Global View

We need to give students at the college level regular opportunity to live and study and work among people of other nations. This should be a normal part of a college education, not merely for a chosen few who can afford it financially, but for a great many and within the normal college fee structure. This is the task of the college or university of today if it is to educate adequately for the life our citizens must live in the future. This is one of the new values which education must emphasize steadily if it is to justify the support and good will it constantly asks from the American people.

Institutions willing to consider an international approach to education should be willing, also, to reconsider the efficacy of the rigid rules and regulations which so frequently bind the curricula. Perhaps such an approach may even help to hasten the day when the difference between an educated and an uneducated man will not be measured by credit course hours, but rather by his attitude and behavior in the world.

(Address at the Seventh Annual Conference of the Council on Student Travel, New York, New York, November 1, 1956)

I

FOR A LONG TIME, I HAVE BEEN CONVINCED OF THE PRIMARY IMportance of a global approach to education as a means to encourage a better understanding of our world and have sought the actual methods by which such an approach could be made feasible for many students. Experience in countries and cultures which differ from our own is one of these methods.

It is important that we state frequently and clearly what our purposes are in encouraging such departures from the more conventional patterns of education. Such reiteration serves to strengthen our own beliefs and perhaps to convert to this cause those who are still doubtful about its merits. Furthermore, I believe it is important that we examine our work with a sense of realism and practicality, recognizing the many problems of technique and method which must be tested to prove the validity of its underlying principles.

II

A wise educator has pointed out that science and technology have annihilated space to a point where it seems as if we are living not so much on a globe as on a globule. The adjustments which man is finding it necessary to make in the evaluation of his place in the world are of tremendous significance.

There is a paradoxical element about such adjustments. On the one hand, man is suddenly more than ever aware of his individual unimportance in the material universe. Dr. Harlow

Shapley, the eminent astronomer, points out that we have now had four adjustments to make in our thinking while we have been acquiring new knowledge about the size of the universe. First, the original concept of the earth-centered universe was supplanted by a second theory of a universe centered on the sun. Then, less than forty years ago, came the necessity for a third adjustment in man's thoughts about his cosmic importance. Through the development of new and more powerful telescopes he discovered what Shapley calls a "galactocentric universe" which puts the earth and its life near the edge of one great galaxy in a universe of millions of galaxies. Finally, today we are faced by an arresting question requiring still another adjustment, perhaps the most difficult of all, the question which asks, "Are we alone?" Knowing that millions of planetary systems must exist, can we suppose that life is restricted merely to the earth? Of course we cannot, says Shapley, and the significance and implications of his conclusions leave the brain reeling.

Directly counter to this astronomical approach is the developing realization in man of his increasing individual importance in shaping the destiny of the world he inhabits. He may be an inhabitant of one out of billions of planets, but the fact is suddenly coming home to him that his survival on his own planet and the betterment of life on that planet are worthy of his most particular and constant consideration. As he discovers what an infinitesimal entity he is in the cosmos, he paradoxically is discovering also that his individual stake in his own world is larger than ever before.

Here in America, we are reminded of this daily as we observe the conduct of our foreign affairs and try to understand the workings of world diplomacy. As the foremost world power, our country has need of the utmost skill and adroitness on the part of its government and people if it is to navigate successfully the dangerous shoals of world tensions. We need the most painstaking awareness of the cultures of other parts of the world, the most penetrating insights into minds foreign to our own, the most compassionate understanding of the problems facing our neighbors throughout the world. It is a new responsibility for America, one which it has not accepted willingly, nor has it fully grasped what is required of itself if as a nation it is to discharge this responsibility with a modicum of success. The results have too often been indifferent successes and even crushing failures.

The social immaturity of our country in foreign relations, which reflects itself often in our dealings with the other powers, is no more than a composite of our individual social immaturity as people. Until we individually know more and understand more about the world, there is little likelihood that our diplomats will do a more effective piece of work. What other nation, for example, would so many times entrust its international affairs, upon which our very existence now depends, to inexperienced representatives who are placed in their positions as rewards for supporting a particular political party and who are so frequently and so summarily removed whenever there is a change of government administration?

The present low state of American prestige abroad is as much the fault of all of us as individual citizens as it is that of our leaders. They can never be too far ahead of us in their thinking, for when they are there is little chance that their policies and decisions will gain wide acceptance among us.

As in so many problems of human life, the answer lies very largely in education. I feel that our school and college curricula need to be more international in their scope, not just for the specialists but for all of us. We need a more comparative view, not only in politics and government and history, but in economics, art, literature, and many other disciplines. In addition to this broader curricular approach, we need to give students at the college level regular opportunity to live and study and work among people of other nations. This should be a normal part of a college education, not merely for a chosen few who can afford it financially, but for a great many and within the normal college fee structure. This is the task of the college or university of today if it is to educate adequately for the life our citizens must live in the future. This is one of the new values which education must emphasize steadily if it is to justify the support and good will it constantly asks from the American people.

III

If we are in agreement that education for tomorrow must be international in character, then the next step is to set forth the basic principles upon which programs of international education should be founded, principles broad enough to encompass the needs and desires of many types of institutions of learning, yet specific enough to be helpful in the formulation of any single program.

The first of seven principles is that of *diversity*. There are many ways to approach a program of international education, and there should be. Just as one of the great strengths of our educational institutions lies in their diversity, the variety of objectives they have, and the highly individualized methods many of them use in working toward those objectives, so a program of international education should be as individualistic as the college or university wishes it to be. It should complement and add power to the already existing educational program. It should be the product of the thinking and planning of the institution itself, geared to its own specific and characteristic needs and representing an extension of the particular philosophy of that institution.

The second major principle is the need for real *breadth of approach* in the consideration of this opportunity. It is important to remember that international education involves not only the component of travel for students, but also matters of curriculum, of intellectual, social, and spiritual values; of understandings of the interrelatedness of man, and of broader interpretation of history.

Our educational processes need to be recast so that their world-wide implications become thoroughly apparent. The study of literature, for example, must expand from the time-honored courses in American and English prose and poetry to include the uniquely beautiful works of writers the world over. It is from such study that we gain clues to the attitudes and values held dear by other cultures and learn to recognize and respect the differences and similarities between those cultures and our own. History, human geography, economics, sociology, government, art, music, and many other fields of knowledge pursued on this broad, comparative basis offer equally penetrating analyses of our world neighbors.

Travel, without the accompanying efforts toward assimilating the cultures of other lands, can be an arid and unrewarding experience. We need only look at the record made by millions of American tourists to see the truth of this. They have demonstrated all too often how possible it is to travel widely and return from the experience with the same insularity and chauvinism they had when they started. Many of them merely transplant geographically their original prejudices and preconceptions and in the process mystify, disturb, and even offend their hosts. Such attitudes help to engender in some of our neighbors the cynicism and cupidity which make the American tourists easy prey as visitors and which they report with such rage when they return.

We need, therefore, the most carefully organized efforts by our colleges and universities to make sure that the travel experience of students is properly reinforced with the broadest and most international kinds of educational approaches, approaches which have their origins on the home campus and which are a steady process, not only for those who will travel, but also for those who will choose to stay at home. The orientation of the student must begin before he goes aboard his ship and is important even if he never goes at all.

Another principle which should undergird this program is the *maintenance of high standards* in all phases of its development. Education abroad is not synonymous with vacation junketing. It is not a way of making education easier or more palatable. On the contrary, it calls forth the highest kind of personal responsibility on the part of the student, for he goes to another country not only to learn but to represent his country and its attitudes to the rest of the world. It is involved with intangible elements which cannot be measured or graded like courses, elements which reflect personality and character. The experiences planned for the student in such a program should be uncompromising in their quality, calling upon him for the utmost in his intellectual, social, and spiritual capacities. They presuppose the most careful kinds of selection among institutions of learning abroad and the most careful planning for any other types of activity. We must never be guilty of the charge that by releasing our students from the conventional classroom or by allowing them to sit in classrooms other than our own we have diluted the strength of the educational process. We should be watchful, rather, that the new and often exotic educational fare we propose to spread before the youth of today and tomorrow will be as rich and nourishing as that which is the pride of our own country.

A fourth principle to guide us is that of *flexibility*. Institutions willing to consider an international approach to education should be willing, also, to reconsider the efficacy of the rigid rules and regulations which so frequently bind the curricula. Perhaps such an approach may even help to hasten the day when the difference between an educated and an uneducated man will not be measured by credit course hours, but rather by his attitudes and behavior in the world.

Recognizing that we must operate within an academic pattern which is well established, we must, none the less, develop a certain elasticity inside such a pattern. Travel, work experience, and study abroad must be gauged fairly for their enriching values and properly estimated to stand in lieu of the more conventional and traditionally charted courses of the normal college catalogue. Such action can come about only with the thorough and sympathetic understanding of faculties, who are in most circumstances reluctant to change the time-honored mores of the academic world. It will be a difficult task, but it can be done. Once the faculty recognizes that flexibility does not mean avoidance of academic responsibility, it will be open to slow persuasion, if not to quick change. It will recognize that a year spent away from the college, a year carefully planned and organized, may be the equal of a year on the campus. It will recognize the intangibles of the maturing process which can so frequently be part of experience abroad and which do not manifest themselves in courses and examinations. It will admit that the creation and nurture of a citizen of the world is an important, if not a vital, educational goal.

The next of seven principles is *financial feasibility*. A program of education abroad must be designed to be within financial reach of the great majority of students who deserve it. Here is the point at which we descend from the lofty realms of abstract dedication to an idea and face the practical and harsh realities of economic possibility. Can education abroad be placed within the reach of many who can afford no more than their regular outlay of money for a college year? Can all the fees, transportation expenses, tuitions, personal costs be kept within the bounds of a normal college year's budget? If they cannot, then we are talking about a program for the few who either have the resources themselves or have them provided through scholarships. Such a program will only touch lightly the objectives we have set for ourselves. If they can, then a new world awaits thousands of students who have never before given serious thought to such possibilities.

Naturally, part of the answer depends upon what the normal costs of a college year happen to be for the individual student. These vary from institution to institution. We all know that tuition fees, for example, are not the same everywhere. In a college, public or private, where such fees are almost nominal, there is little question that the student would find it difficult to budget a year abroad within the total limits of his normal expenditures. Great numbers of our colleges and universities today, however, have tuition fees which are relatively large and growing even larger. In such institutions there should be no financial problem for the student who desires experience in a foreign land.

There is enough evidence to warrant an extensive experiment and to indicate good chances for success. True, we shall have to limit operations at first, but the passage of time may bring new attitudes on the part of those in control of air and sea transportation, so that the Orient, Africa, and South America will not be beyond our reach. The Council on Student Travel is and will be an important factor in bringing these attitudes about.

Let us remember, also, as we think of this principle that it includes the self-sustaining element. Although a subsidy may be necessary to launch the program and maintain it in its early stages, eventually the program must support itself as well as any other phase of a college's educational program; at least, it must not add greatly to the total burden which every college carries today and will continue to carry for years to come.

The principle of financial feasibility is not as frightening or unrealistic as many suppose it to be. It merely presupposes prudence, careful organization, and a real desire on the part of the student to make of his time abroad a meaningful and educationally enriching experience.

The sixth principle is *continuity*. This involves the development of a program long-range in its view and ever-expanding in its possibilities. Once an institution embarks upon a program of international education, it must stay with it long enough to give it every chance to succeed. There should be provision for steady growth year after year as the program proves its merit, and there should be willingness to accept the occasional failures and setbacks without faltering from the main purpose. If one method or the experience in one country turns out badly, this in itself should not be allowed to break the series of efforts which together form a continuing pattern. We shall have to be patient in evaluating results, for they will not be easy to measure nor will they be evident quickly. All the more reason, then, for continuity and the long view.

Our final concern is with the principle of *thorough interpretation*. It is not enough for us to devise a good program if very few know about it or understand it. Not only must parents, students, and faculty be fully aware of all its purposes and details, but other educational institutions, travel agencies, business, and industry must realize the true significance of its outreach. Thus, the most careful kind of interpretative activities must be undertaken. Only in this way can the idea of international education permeate the thinking and even the support of all our citizenry.

Parents will see in such an idea the exciting opportunities for having their children assimilate a world point of view and the broadest kinds of cultural enrichment. Students will discover new and more distant horizons, new and more far-flung career possibilities, as well as a close and intimate relationship with a larger physical and spiritual world. Faculty will see new avenues to explore in learning and in understanding and will find added satisfactions stemming from the global aspects of their subject matter and teaching methods. Travel agencies will see, beyond the commercial potentials of their enterprises, a service motive in their work which makes them true partners in the process of encouraging and stimulating education. Business and industry will be aware, also, of *their* place in this partnership between education and the rest of life, realizing that besides encouraging our youth to look for careers on all the continents, and thus providing staff members adequately trained and oriented, they are basing their economic progress upon true human understanding.

To interpret this idea so universally, not only to people in this country, but also to their counterparts abroad, will not be an easy or quick task. It will not be accepted without real opposition from those who still long for the insular and self-sufficient attitudes of the past. This is all the more reason to make a beginning and to pledge ourselves to a long and tedious period of labor with all the attendant frustrations. Understanding and acceptance will inevitably come, if we are persevering and effective in translating our purposes.

These seven principles for a program of international education, obvious as they may seem, can make the difference between success and failure. Diversity, breadth of approach, maintenance of high standards, flexibility, financial feasibility, continuity, and thorough interpretation—here are guidelines in an exciting and fascinating project aimed toward the achievement of the most elusive, yet most necessary, goals of man. Mutual understanding and compassion on the part of each individual, leading to a world peace buttressed not only by international laws and treaties but by true largeness of heart—here are the goals we so earnestly seek. They are worthy of our most strenuous efforts.

13

The Sinews of Learning

The purposes and objectives of a liberal arts college using co-operative education are not perceptibly different from those of the more conventional institution. They are to develop mature, effective members of society endowed with a sense of independence and responsibility. The differences are those of method, not of purpose, representing different means to the same end. The co-operative program in the liberal arts college actually strengthens and enhances the liberal arts and field course content of the curriculum in a number of ways.

❧ ❧ ❧

One of the most cogent arguments for the work-study plan is that it is a major practical step toward the solution of two of our most pressing educational problems, namely the need for more facilities and more faculty to take care of additional millions of students.

❧ ❧ ❧

In the concept of co-operative education there is a meeting ground for educators and businessmen on which they can stand and work together with the sure knowledge that out of this unified effort can come an important contribution to the future well-being of our people.

(Address at the Thomas Alva Edison Foundation Conference on Co-operative Education and the Impending Educational Crisis, Dayton, Ohio, May 23, 1957)

I

WE ALL RECOGNIZE THAT IN SPITE OF THE DIVERSITY NOW existing in American higher education, the conventional patterns of the past are a strong deterrent to experimentation in educational ideas. This has always been true and is no less true today. Even though we are being warned and reminded daily of the swarms of college-age students which are about to descend upon us, even though we realize that our facilities and faculties will be inadequate for meeting these new demands, even though we see glaring weaknesses in the way we have organized and carried on the learning process for many years, we cling nostalgically and sometimes almost pathetically to the ways of the past because we know them, and they are comfortable and reassuring by the mere fact that we have followed them so long.

I do not have the temerity or folly to suggest that the answer to all our educational problems of the future lies in co-operative education. There are many answers to these problems depending on many factors, but I *do* suggest that some form of co-operative education, partial or complete, broad or limited, can be of significant assistance to colleges and universities of all types as they grapple with their individual difficulties. I *do* suggest that co-operative education merits consideration by liberal arts colleges, as well as by technical institutions or departments. I *do* suggest that co-operative education should not be ignored when one deliberates on the academic, financial, and administrative enhancement of a program of higher education. I suggest these things, for Antioch College is an institution which has proved since 1921 that such a program is not only possible and practical but desirable.

A study made a few years ago of a comparative sampling of ten-year graduates of Antioch and those of a more conventional liberal arts college of outstanding quality (a study entered upon by mutual agreement and with mutual confidence) disclosed a number of provocative and almost startling facts. These were two institutions whose only true major difference lay in the circumstance that in one there was no co-operative education, and in the other it was a requirement for everyone. Over thirty separate items were checked by the alumni of the two colleges, items of fact rather than opinion. In virtually every one of the items, the Antioch alumni showed more progress, although on many of the items the difference between them and the other alumni was statistically insignificant. For example, the income of the Antioch graduate was materially higher, about $1000 a year higher.

Some items *were* significant. The Antioch graduate had chosen his career more quickly, and what is more important, was happier with his choice. His sense of civic responsibility appeared stronger in terms of the extent of his regular activities in the community where he lived. These are a few of the results. I mention them to dispel whatever impression may exist that a college with a co-operative education plan dilutes the quality of its product. The very opposite can be true if the institution insists upon high and uncompromising standards.

II

I should like to outline six broad principles which should undergird any program of co-operative education, in the hope that by so doing I can show its feasibility for institutions of many types, including the liberal arts college. Any mention of Antioch in this process will be more than coincidental, simply because these are the principles by which it functions and with which it has had a considerable degree of success.

The first principle on which co-operative education should be based is *high academic quality*. Many times the only reasons offered in favor of such a plan are its values toward choosing a vocation and the possibilities it presents for earning one's way through college. In terms of a liberal arts college approach, these two reasons are only by-products of the plan and are not necessarily its major assets. The purposes and objectives of a liberal arts college using co-operative education are not perceptibly different from those of the more conventional institution. They are to develop mature, effective members of society endowed with a sense of independence and responsibility. The differences are those of method, not of purpose, representing different means to the same end. The co-operative program in the liberal arts college actually strengthens and enhances the liberal arts and field course content of the curriculum in a number of ways.

It strengthens the course content by its practical observation in the field of much that is discussed theoretically in the classroom. The student sees directly what actually is being done and how it is being done. Often he has the experience of actually doing it. Such practical observation or experience by the student has the effect of making the professor more alert to contemporary circumstances. Knowing that he will be challenged by the student who has just returned from the field, he is more inclined to keep himself up-to-date and abreast of developments in his subject matter area. Here is real interaction between work and study which gives practical overtones to sound theory.

The co-operative approach adds another human dimension to the liberal arts program, since it expands the walls of the classroom to include the outside world. It offers regular contacts with adults off the campus—employers, alumni, friends—and by those contacts opens ways to better understanding of human relationships. It takes a long stride into adulthood, yet not such a stride that youth is lost and campus life disappears. It speeds up the process of maturation by its impact upon the personality or personal development of the student. It encourages a sense of responsibility in the student which adds to his versatility and adaptability in a variety of situations. It strengthens his sense of social consciousness through direct experience with a wide range of social patterns, communities, and value systems. As one Antioch student expressed it in one of his major papers:

> With increasing social interaction one comes to realize the necessity for versatility in differing social situations, if one desires to be effective. For example, the persons with whom you are in daily contact on jobs are sometimes not those whom you would choose as associates, given the freedom of choice. Nevertheless, to facilitate accomplishment and to maintain the necessary professional relationships, there must be mutual accommodation to common areas of interest and discussion.

This student had job experiences in Ohio, Texas, Idaho, Colorado, and Wisconsin.

I cannot emphasize too strongly the values of co-operative education as an experience in living, quite aside from its other values. It is a venture into maturity with all the accompanying vexing problems and thrilling awakenings. Coming into a strange community, meeting new people including an employer and working associates, living within a budget on money earned by oneself, searching for cultural aspects of one's environment to fill up the leisure hours, handling one's own travel arrangements—these and other experiences are dramatic foreshadowings of how one will live as an adult, tentative but vital steps in learning to walk as a mature and poised man or woman. Rather amazing metamorphoses take place frequently during the total college career as the student goes out and returns again and again.

Still another way by which co-operative education contributes to the academic strength of the undergraduate program is in its fostering of the concept of continuing education. The student learns very clearly that cultural or intellectual pursuits and vocational interests are equal parts of life. Having dealt with both in parallel fashion during college years, he has captured some notion of this concept of life-long education and is inclined to accept its inclusion in his plans as part of a regular and normal pattern for living.

The academic content of a college education can actually be enhanced, therefore, through the application of a broadly conceived and properly motivated co-operative program which sees its purposes stretching far beyond the vocational or financial.

A second principle on which a proper plan of co-operative education should be based is that of *individualized assistance*. Adhering to this principle means that each student, in order to derive maximum benefit from his program, should be helped individually in his choice of work opportunities, in developing his academic directions, and generally in shaping his college career. There cannot be a mass approach in co-operative education. If there were, its true values would disappear.

At Antioch with its 1100 students, a staff of ten full-time professional people, referred to as the "Personnel Department," counsel students for the jobs to which they seem fitted, search out employers and develop contacts with them, place students in jobs according to their needs and abilities, visit employers and students while the latter are in the field in order to ascertain their progress. The department fulfills these duties, plus the scrutiny of job reports sent in by students and employers, general counseling, and routine maintenance of proper records. Each department member has been chosen because of his special knowledge of a particular field as well as his general attributes as a counselor. In the course of the student's college career, he comes to know his personnel director well. The employers who deal with the personnel director also come to know him well and learn to rely upon his judgments in sending students to them.

The personnel director is the key to the success or failure of the co-operative program. His ability to size up the student correctly and to match him to the proper series of jobs, plus his ability to search out meaningful job opportunities and to convince employers of the advantages which accrue from their participation is the real strength upon which the program rests. He handles the students assigned to him in completely individual fashion, not according to a general group pattern.

Through individualized assistance, the program inevitably acquires an element of flexibility. Since there are no rigid patterns to follow and since each student is considered in terms of his individual need, a considerable number of varying approaches to the work-study problem develop. Sometimes a student works two consecutive periods because of the peculiar nature of the job; sometimes he finds a job himself and requires only the checking by the personnel director to make sure it will have within it the elements which make it worthwhile; sometimes he returns to the same job several times, although more often he returns only once; sometimes he interrupts the regular work-study pattern to have a year abroad in some other college or university. The program is flexible, yet it adheres to very specific standards of time spent in work and study and the quality of achievement.

Another result of individualized assistance is that the college must necessarily remain small to operate such a program successfully. Let us interpret the word "small" to mean a college of 1200 or less. While one could multiply the number of personnel directors in a large institution, experience seems to indicate that all sorts of complications set in. A reasonably-sized department within a large university is, of course, quite capable of carrying on such a program. But any characteristic of an institution which would indicate insensitivity to individual need and guidance would mitigate against the possibilities of real success. Basically, the co-operative program is suited to the small college or small department in a university. In such an atmosphere individualized assistance and program flexibility are more readily obtainable.

The third principle on which a co-operative program is built is that of *independent action.* It is obvious that the success of any work-study arrangement depends to a very large extent upon the kinds of relationships developed between the college and the many employers who agree to participate. It must be a relationship which is close enough to insure truly mutual understanding. On the college's part there is a commitment to select students for jobs who will be adequate to the tasks and will fit reasonably into the organization alongside the permanent employees. On the employer's side is a commitment to be what Antioch calls a "field faculty member," someone concerned enough about the future of young men and women to look upon their presence in his organization as a creative and worthwhile experience for them. He is willing to evaluate their work, report on their progress, even to counsel them from time to time. In such a capacity, he is an extension of the regular faculty.

In addition to these individual commitments by college and employer, there is a set of mutual commitments which have nothing directly to do with the student. It is these which have to do more specifically with the principle of independent action. They involve the guarantee of no *quid pro quo* on either side. The college should not look upon the employer as one who will be sent students in proportion to his willingness to offer general financial support to the institution. Similarly, the employer should not expect to be able to obtain students on such a basis, or with the understanding that the students who come to him will eventually become his permanent employees. Such understanding between college and employer does not rule out the latter as a possible contributor, nor does it prohibit the students from seeking permanent positions with their co-operative employers. It merely assures that any such actions are independent in character and are not the result of pressures applied by either side.

At Antioch, in the normal course of events, financial assistance is not solicited from the more than four hundred employers with whom the college deals regularly. When such assistance is received, it stems from an independent feeling on the part of the employer that he wishes to help the institution. The co-operative arrangement with him has nothing to do with the possibility of his financial support, and the college does not enter into agreements which guarantee that any student will become a permanent employee. When this occurs, it is because the student wishes it after, and only after, his experience with the organization makes such a course of action desirable to him.

The essential freedoms of an academic institution must be protected and maintained regardless of the type of program it establishes for itself or the methods of education it uses. Such freedoms should never be endangered by financial considerations either for the college or its students. A college is not a propagandizing or promotional agency; it is a place for the free exploration of ideas on all subjects, impartially presented and openly discussed with due attention and weight given to human experience as a basis for judging the validity of such ideas.

Another principle essential to a co-operative program is that under normal circumstances there should be *financial remuneration to the student* for the work he performs. This may seem to be an obvious or even inconsequential point, but in actuality it is neither. Part of the value of the co-operative program lies in having the student earn money and live on the money he earns. This is an important living experience. It has nothing to do with whether the student has financial need or whether he is in financially independent circumstances. There is value in his realization of what his work is worth. Thus, the usual arrangement between college and employer should include an understanding that the employer will pay whatever wage normally attaches to the particular job. The fact that the worker is a student should make no difference, for it is expected that sufficient demands will be made upon him to warrant the payment of the wage. In this regard, sentiment has no place. The student is not paid out of the goodness of the employer's heart. He earns what he receives. The student must learn early that the world does not pay people out of sentiment but for value received.

Antioch has occasional instances in which a student has a particular desire for work for some agency which cannot afford to take on additional expense, even though it could use his services. This is allowed from time to time, although it is not encouraged. A student entering into such an arrangement does so with full understanding of the unusual character of his job and its rather unrealistic quality. Such a job can and does sometimes offer a unique opportunity for broad educational growth and, therefore, is not completely ruled out. In general, however, the basic principle outlined is the one adhered to.

Another aspect of this principle, frequently misunderstood, is the general belief that co-operative education is designed primarily as a means by which the student earns his way through college. This is not a basic assumption in the Antioch program, although it is at least a partial by-product. Through his earnings the student may assist himself in paying his college expenses, but most of his earnings will probably cover only his transportation and living expenses while on the job. As he matures and takes on positions of more responsibility, he may in fact be able to save out of his earnings. A program based entirely on such a premise, however, has latent dangers in it, dangers to the total educative process which is the real and only truly valid reason for its existence. The financial burden of the student may be lightened, but it is rarely, if ever, lifted entirely. At Antioch, as in all other educational institutions, it is necessary to provide scholarship aid and loans to help needy students toward the fruition of their educational plans. The student should be able to go wherever the proper job opportunity presents itself, even if it takes him halfway across the country. If he thinks only of earning his way through college, he will tend to limit the scope of his exploration. Antioch students are in approximately thirty states as well as abroad, and this is a normal situation.

The fifth principle for a sound co-operative education program is one of *economy*. One of the most cogent arguments for the work-study plan is that it is a major practical step toward the solution of two of our most pressing educational problems, namely the need for more facilities and more faculty to take care of additional millions of students. Let me illustrate specifically what I mean by describing the situation at Antioch College.

Not more than about 650 of the total enrollment of 1,100 students are on campus at one time because of the work-study arrangement. Physical facilities are planned to take care of this on-campus contingent, not the total enrollment. Similarly, a full-time faculty of sixty-five is involved with 650 students at a time, and thus maintains a teacher-student ratio of one to ten. The same dormitories, classrooms, library, dining facilities, gymnasiums, and laboratories serve both of the alternating student bodies, as does the same faculty. The process of shifting at the end of each twelve-week period may be considered by some to be complicated, but students have experienced this kind of shifting for years without feeling unduly put upon. The faculty plans its courses in somewhat different fashion, but no dilution of course content results from this. With one of the four periods of the year free for vacation, the faculty teaching year is about the same as anywhere else. The teaching loads each period compare favorably with those at other liberal arts institutions.

In considering economy, one must remember that under the co-operative plan at Antioch a personnel department consisting of a number of professional and clerical staff is necessary. It is true that this is a department not found in the conventional college, because it is unnecessary there. It is also true that operating this department requires a considerable portion of funds available annually for college expenses. At Antioch, the Personnel Department has a budget of almost $100,000. But even with this unusual expenditure, the total cost of the college program is considerably below what it would be if one had to make provision for the full complement of students at the same time on the campus.

Everywhere colleges are struggling to erect new buildings and to expand faculties as they view the impending crisis. Yet here is a way to make fuller use of already existing facilities and personnel; in fact, student bodies may even be doubled within present campus facilities—and all without endangering the quality of the academic process. Here is a way to operate with more efficiency and economy and to show businessmen and industrialists whom we ask to support us that we have done everything we can to make every dollar stretch to its utmost before we plead for additional funds. Most of all, here is a way in which the very pattern itself reduces spoon-feeding and coddling to a minimum and encourages self-reliant and responsible qualities of the student.

If we wish our students to be self-reliant, mature, and responsible, then we as institutions of higher learning must set an example of similar self-reliance and responsibility in the way we operate. We have no right to speak critically of the tendency of the younger generation to be security-minded and unadventurous when we ourselves appear unwilling to meet our present crisis boldly and decisively. We must innovate and experiment and combine and revise and prune and reorganize until we have found better and more economical methods and techniques academically and administratively. Having done this, we have a right to ask for the fullest and most sympathetic support from alumni and business and industry and foundations and individual philanthropists. And having done this, we can expect to receive such support.

The final principle involved in a co-operative program is actually common to all educational programs. It is the necessity for *continuity of interpretation*. Not enough is known in this country today about co-operative education, and much of what is known is misinterpreted or misunderstood. Antioch is deeply sensitive to this, for after thirty-six years under a work-study plan it still learns of odd misconceptions of what it is doing or why. The blame for this rests in the apparent failure to make known with accuracy and completeness the nature of the program offered and the benefits it affords.

It would seem reasonable to insist, therefore, that it is not enough to devise and put into practice a co-operative program which is effective educationally. It must be explained and interpreted over and over again, even to those who are participating in it as well as to the many and varied publics beyond the campus. Its characteristics and values need constant exposition to parents, communities, business and service organizations, potential and actual employers, educational and lay leaders. Repeated assurances must be given of the academic quality, the educational depth, the potential for personality growth and vocational knowledge, and all the other positive elements which such a program, properly organized and administered, can supply to the youth of America. Communication is the first basic step toward an understanding of the purposes of co-operative education, and such communication should go on uninterruptedly with every means and resource the college can muster.

III

In essence, then: it is entirely possible and even desirable for a college, liberal arts or technical in character and undergraduate in level, to operate within a co-operative education pattern; and six principles, I feel, are essential to the success of such a pattern. This explanation of principles has inevitably developed some sort of picture of what a co-operative program is in its functioning and its characteristics.

The days ahead are days of remarkable opportunity for American higher education and for American business and industry. They are remarkable for the former in that they open broader educational horizons than have ever been envisaged before, horizons which reach far beyond the conventional and unfulfilling patterns of today. They are remarkable for the latter in that they offer new realizations to business and industry of their stake in higher education, both to assure the continuing progress of their own enterprises and to guarantee a strong, educated, humane citizenry for our country. In the concept of co-operative education there is a meeting ground for educators and businessmen on which they can stand and work together with the sure knowledge that out of this unified effort can come an important contribution to the future well-being of our people. Rightly conceived and properly executed, the co-operative education approach is the basis for a partnership long overdue on the American scene.

14

Fanning the Embers

No one claims that democracy has developed a race of whole men; but democracy, better than any other form of government yet devised, furnishes the climate in which whole men may develop, in which men may fulfill their inner reason for being. Education is a bulwark in the fight for the development of the whole man, and adult education is one of its strengthening timbers.

⸍ ⸍ ⸍

There is more than promise and hope ahead for the many and diverse patterns of post-high school education. There is an impelling necessity. The leisure-time activities of increasing millions of our citizens, especially as they reach retirement age, the vast amount of time to be filled by housewives whose families have grown up and left the home, the minds of millions of men and women who do not go to college out of choice or circumstance, as well as the millions who do—all these present ample material with which we can and must employ ourselves.

(Address at the Twentieth Annual Conference of the Ohio Association for Adult Education, Columbus, Ohio, March 21, 1958)

I

NEVER BEFORE IN AMERICA HAVE SO MANY PEOPLE OF VARIED walks of life or so many institutions and agencies of varying types been so much involved with those post-war patterns of education which are less formal in nature, those which are not the normal patterns of higher education as found in our colleges and universities, those which we have come to label "adult education." Several millions of adults can be arranged statistically along with hundreds upon hundreds of institutions in terms of the educational courses or activities in which they are regularly engaged. Such a statistical result is heartwarming and encouraging. Yet we can with equal truth point to many more millions of people and thousands of institutions and agencies who have not yet involved themselves at all. The great deal which has been accomplished, the great progress to which we can point, the great upsurge of interest in adult education—these are only preliminary to the task yet remaining to be performed.

We stand today in full recognition of two of the elementary facts of educational life for the future. By simple mathematics we know that the numbers of pupils in our schools and colleges will double or perhaps even triple in the next twenty years. We know, also, that the regular channels of formal education at all levels are bound to be almost hopelessly clogged as the increasing numbers of students overwhelm our inadequate facilities and our short supply of qualified teachers. In the face of this sobering knowledge we would show little surprise and perspicacity if we did not bethink ourselves of more informal, unstructured possibilities in education for adults of all ages who will inevitably be shut out of our institutions of higher learning but who are as thirsty for knowledge and as needful of broad human understanding as their more fortunate counterparts.

We would show little wisdom if we neglected to recognize that ignoramuses are dangerous in the world of tomorrow, as much or more so than they are today, and that new realizations of man's place in the scientific and humanistic world must be developed for millions upon millions, many of whom will not find their way into our colleges and universities. The question today is not so much the one being bandied about so freely, "Who shall go to college?" It is rather the question, "Who shall not be educated to the fullest degree of his capacity to learn?" This is a matter not just for schools and colleges to ponder; it is a matter for an entire citizenry and its congeries of family groups, its church boards, its social and cultural activity leaders, its mass media, its librarians, its farm bureau agents, its labor union leaders, its museum directors, its park and forest authorities; in short, it is a matter of concern for every facet of human life, organized and unorganized.

The second elementary fact of educational life is equally arresting. On October 5, 1957, we entered a new era comparable in its world-shaking effect to the atomic era we entered in 1942 and to a few other eras of the past. In some ways the entrance into the space age is the most tremendous happening of all, for it adds a dimension to life hitherto assigned by most men to the realm of fantasy. All education, including adult education, must be alert to the significance of this new dimension, for it places new strictures upon us all. Oddly enough, these are not merely the strictures brought about by the need for more science and more mathematics. They are, rather, those which make all the more impelling the need for men of good will in the world. The path that education provides must be to new understandings of the divine spark in man which gives meaning to his place in the universe. The real problem for education is not the development of scientific theories and tools, but rather the creation of spiritual strength and social consciousness in the soul of man.

II

Perhaps I can best illustrate one of my main points by a little-known story about Mark Twain. He was an inveterate buyer of new gadgets, and while living in Hartford he was one of the first subscribers to that new gadget, the telephone.

Twain had managed to conceal from Mrs. Twain the fact that in her absence he exercised his magnificent repertoire of profanity, gathered from those most eloquent cursers, the Mississippi River pilots. The quality of the telephone service in those early days offered ample opportunity to such talents, since tempers were constantly being riled by wrong numbers and interruptions of service.

On one occasion when Mark Twain was particularly exasperated by the failure of the gadget, he burned the balky wires with his richest river invective. Hanging up with a grand flourish, he turned and to his surprise saw Mrs. Twain standing there, cold-faced and aloof.

Perhaps Mrs. Twain had been taught by her mother that the way to cure a husband of profanity was to join him in the pastime. Then he would realize how horrible it sounded and would be properly ashamed. And so, in rather halting but unmistakable words, Mrs. Twain repeated her husband's telephone comments verbatim.

Mark Twain looked at her for a long time admiringly but rather regretfully. Then shaking his head, he said, "My dear, you have all the words but none of the music."

If I were to characterize the past history of adult education in America and much of its present, I would suggest that it has always had the words but rarely the music. This is not said in derogation of the magnificent work done over the years by the pioneers of such an educational movement. Indeed, they did first things first, as they should have done, but the music of adult education which intrigues me in its present and future is the spirit with which it should be permeated and the concept by which it should be developed. The spirit is identified by a creative urge which has its impact upon people searching for a finer life and for individual maturity. The concept is that of education as a continuing process, a never-ending process in life. It is a concept geared to the active, inquiring mind, stored with the harvest of study and experience but aware that a full consummation of anything never takes place. As Charles Kettering has said, "We never arrive in this world; we are transients in time."

The past of the adult education movement in this country is sometimes difficult to interpret, but some elements are relatively clear. One is that there has been much more emphasis upon *learning in order to earn* than upon *learning in order to live and grow*. The lion's share of adult education courses has been in the skill or vocational areas and in the preparation of aliens for citizenship. Indeed, it was by this latter type of course that adult education frequently tiptoed its way into public school system budgets. In more recent years a second emphasis has been felt, namely that which stressed the avocational or "hobby" courses, designed in most cases for relaxation of the mind. Only in the last few decades has there been any widespread recognition that adult education must reach into the humanities as a resource and must turn itself to the task so inherent in a democracy, the task of seeing to it that people are whole men rather than half men.

In a world where visible success has become the high god, the sole pursuit of this success results in half men, men so completely absorbed in the externals of life that the inner man, the important half of man, is left to wither. The world revolution is deeper than a material world being turned upside down. It is the people of the world being turned inside out. It is the fight between the outer man and the inner man. It is a struggle in which one side seeks to control the mind, the other to set it free. It must be waged everywhere. The fight will not be won with H-bombs and guided missiles and the launching of satellites. Superiority in such a fight may merely preserve our bodies for a while. It will be won in men's hearts, where understanding has been nurtured by a steady and unceasing process of education, the kind of education that makes men whole.

No one claims that democracy has developed a race of whole men; but democracy, better than any other form of government yet devised, furnishes the climate in which whole men may develop, in which men may fulfill their inner reason for being. Education is a bulwark in the fight for the development of the whole man, and adult education is one of its strengthening timbers.

III

For a long time many have chosen to identify adult education with an almost fundamentalist approach. The concept has been largely one of courses—courses offered by many kinds of institutions, courses in citizenship, how-to-do-it courses, extension courses, credit courses toward a degree, credit courses in liberal arts, non-credit courses in liberal arts, etc. The classroom or the laboratory or the workshop and the teacher have been considered essential parts of the adult educational pattern. Probably this comes about because of our passion in America for order and organization, as well as our unwillingness to break away from well-worn patterns in formal education to which we are all accustomed. The idea of learning anything without taking a course is a difficult one for some people to adjust to. The idea of learning anything without the ever-present guidance of a teacher is equally difficult for some to encompass.

Now I would not argue against the value of courses as a pattern of adult education. As a matter of fact, I would readily agree to their importance and probable validity whatever their type or level of purpose. But I *would* argue that adult education has many other patterns, wider patterns with tremendously significant meaning for the individual, and that, therefore, the proper conception of adult education is a much more inclusive and broad one. Such a concept recognizes that adult education includes many kinds of exposure to all sorts of educational influences in drama, art, music, dance, or literature by means of theatres, libraries, museums, television, radio, films, and magazines—to name only some. Such a concept recognizes the day-to-day influence of all these elements and seeks to use them wisely and educatively in whatever form or setting they present themselves. It also recognizes that if the desire to learn all through a lifetime is to be established and encouraged, it must be established during childhood and youth. It must be a part of the early formal learning process if it is ever to carry over into the more informal in later life.

It is preoccupation with this broader conception of adult education which has led Antioch College into a somewhat unorthodox approach. Incomplete and unproven as it may be, this program is an example, not necessarily of excellence, but of effort to translate this conception into action.

The very fact that Antioch is so much involved in what it calls "continuing education" is unorthodox enough, I suppose. Not too many small liberal arts colleges feel this area to be of great concern to them except as it may relate directly to their formal program. At Antioch, having a concern for continuing education is quite natural, for the co-operative or work-study plan which all undergraduate students follow is predicated on the same concept. It is our belief that vocational and cultural interests should develop in parallel fashion all through life and that education is ever a part of man's existence and growth. The college experience of our students with both study and work drive this point home to them unmistakably and sets the pattern for their adulthood.

Adult education at Antioch already has many facets to it

and is expected to have more. The more orthodox are the Adult Education Center which offers to the community non-credit courses with considerable emphasis on the liberal arts and special credit courses for science and mathematics teachers of the area. An interesting development in this Center has been the introduction of courses for the whole family as a unit, beginning with French and adding literature and science. Special lectures are also offered to the alumni in their own communities and on campus at Commencement time.

Less conventional, however, is Antioch's interpretation of adult education to include the activities of a Summer Shakespeare Festival visited by 167,000 people over a six-year period. These people viewed all the works of Shakespeare, as well as a few others, an experience of tremendous cultural value. Other summer activities include concerts, a writers' conference, and eventually work and exhibitions in the art field and the dance. Already built and in operation is a camp for elementary school children where they may live with their teachers and study the conservation and development of natural resources, a camp which is in use for adult groups on weekends throughout the year and even more widely during the summer. In an attempt to discover techniques by which to develop the concept of continuing education in young children Antioch initiates experiments in its own demonstration school which goes through the sixth grade. Finally, an FM educational radio station has been opened to serve the geographic area with programming largely designed to stimulate educational and cultural interests of the community.

I shall not pause to describe some of the specific program plans or processes which are further reflections of the broad conception of adult education I am advocating. I wish merely to establish the point that, in my opinion, such a broad conception is desirable and necessary if we are to meet the demands of the future. Twelve principles upon which effective programs of adult education should be based are listed here:

1. *A broad conception of educational purposes and broad means by which to achieve these purposes.*

It is important to conceive of adult education through every possible influence, formal and informal, structured and unstructured. When this is done, new vistas of opportunity are opened and means present themselves for use. Some may argue that I am dealing more in semantics than in policy development and am merely claiming every cultural activity as adult education without really making any original contribution. This I would deny, for I believe that the broad approach I am recommending will give new meaning and new direction to each activity and will cause its pattern to change in order to accommodate itself to the total concept. For example, there is a difference between a series of concerts, given as such, and a series of concerts built around an educational theme and buttressed by supporting activities to strengthen the educational point. Similar examples could be offered in drama, dance, art exhibits, television, discussions, book fairs, etc. All that is required is a belief in this conception plus some ingenuity and breadth of imagination.

2. *Sound relationships with permanent institutions.*

Adult education should have an organizational anchor which insures against the possibility of its drifting away into oblivion as the tide of its popularity occasionally recedes. All too often a program is begun by the creation of a special agency. This is designed to co-ordinate or give leadership to the program and to guarantee the sympathetic support and, if possible, the participation of local civic and educational groups. Such action is praiseworthy, of course, but inherently dangerous by itself. If the program is to last, if it is to survive the vicissitudes of time and circumstance, then its most important connection and the real initiative for its existence must come from a permanent institution in the area, and preferably one identified by a deep concern for fostering liberal education. The public schools are an example, but a college or university is an even better one.

The college or university has the advantages of more direct experience with education, more prestige as a result of this direct experience, more concern with long-range or even timeless goals, more access to skilled personnel, more basic facilities and support to launch a program, more aptitude for adapting methods it already knows to the peculiar needs of adult education, more staying power in the face of adverse circumstances during the early days of the venture, more likelihood as an institution to recognize its responsibility to the total community, more breadth or catholicity in its approach, more opportunity to co-ordinate wisely the diverse and diffuse elements of every community. This does not mean that every college or university will utilize these advantages, but under ordinary circumstances it is the natural initiator and co-ordinator, if it chooses to be. It can help without dominating and by its help can guarantee a permanence to the program equal or almost equal to its own.

3. *Utilization of all community resources.*

Using a college or university to spearhead the development of an adult education program does not in any way rule out the utilization of every other resource of the community. One of the first steps in creating a program is that of census-taking—listing and examining the agencies, the social, religious, and cultural institutions of the area with some evaluation of how their present activities can fit into the projected pattern; searching for potential leadership among lay citizens both for organizational and educational purposes; studying the physical facilities whether public buildings, private homes, recreational developments, or even space in industrial plants; evaluating the potential interest in participation or support for the program. From such a census can come practical realizations regarding the degree of complexity the program may be able to cope with successfully and the speed with which it can be developed. Without this kind of information carefully collected and interpreted, there is danger of haphazard design and ultimate breakdown.

4. *Local sovereignty and grass roots participation in planning.*

Closely linked with the principle of utilizing the resources of the community is the equally important necessity for calling upon the local citizenry from the very beginning for advice and assistance in shaping the program's design. The adult education program must meet the needs and desires of the local community, or it has no reason for being. It is bound to have individual and distinctive characteristics caused by such needs and desires; it cannot be the exact counterpart of programs in progress elsewhere. Most of all, it cannot be a program brought in from elsewhere and fashioned by strangers. It must rather be the result of co-operative effort by many local citizens representing many differing interests and points of view. There are a number of ways to accomplish this kind of climate for program development. One, for example, is the formation of an advisory council of reasonable size, consisting of individuals chosen for their ability and interest who work with representatives of the permanent institution not only in the initiation of the program but regularly thereafter. Antioch has found such a council to be the key element for progress and the balancing factor preventing the program from being overweighted on any side. It examines policy and leaves details to its director. Furthermore, it is a major device for communicating quickly and directly with the community. Another approach is to create a council of representatives from various segments of the community life who serve because of their position.

The important thing to remember is the fostering of an attitude that the community itself is determining what it is going to do and that its program will therefore be peculiarly its own, with the specific and characteristic stamp of that community upon it. We have long championed the ideal of diversity in formal education; the same principle is equally desirable in adult education.

5. *Non-compartmentalization of knowledge.*

I plead for this principle in adult education because of what the lack of its application has done to the American school system generally. Our tendency to section off areas of knowledge, dividing them into thinner and thinner portions, has resulted in loss of a total perspective in terms of the whole range of knowledge. Specialization has become a fetish not only in professional education, where it may have a certain validity, but even in the liberal arts and other undergraduate studies. There is danger of the same thing happening in adult education if we are not careful. It can be prevented if we develop knowledge and appreciation by other than formal course methods; it can also be prevented if we shape the courses we present to encompass more than a single discipline and to be related directly to the larger and less specialized problems of life. This cannot be done at every level, but it can be striven for as the adult student's attention can be gradually drawn to broader and more basic elements that constitute real education. In a way, I am arguing for fewer courses and more activities, but I have no illusions about how strong the demand will be for courses. Still, a course in agriculture can well be as much involved with economics, foreign affairs, domestic politics, and psychology as with crop development, if I interpret my newspapers correctly.

6. *Emphasis upon discussion techniques.*

In a democratic society we must have an articulate as well as an intelligent citizenry if we are to prosper. Our ability to communicate with one another, to exchange ideas, to offer opinions, to discuss logically and effectively are inherent necessities in our education. We face the realistic fact that a great portion of our people have never been trained in these abilities. Formal education has too many times neglected this important aspect of preparation for life. It behooves us, therefore, to make certain that our programs of adult education provide ample and regular opportunities for the development of skill in discussion. No matter what the subject matter, in most instances the techniques of discussion can most easily and effectively make our people think. They can offer an informal, pleasant, and productive method for learning, a method which is an integral part of the democratic life. An adult education program should be organized around discussion, carefully planned, skilfully led, and practiced through participation by every student.

7. *Establishment of means for regular training of leadership.*

Discussion techniques are not normally acquired by accident. They are the result of training which must precede many courses to be offered. This means that willing and likely discussion leaders must be sought in the community and that they must be given sufficient preparation in the fundamentals of these techniques. It means also that such training is a continuing process in any adult education program, since new courses and activities need to be led and new leaders need to be recruited. The fastest deterioration of a program comes through failure to find leaders and train them. Fortunately, the development of good discussion leaders is not a difficult or overlong process in most communities once the proper organization is created to find those potentially capable, to interest them, and to give them the knowledge and encouragement they require. The natural interests of people uncover many splendid prospects who, as they gain experience, feel a new sense of achievement and satisfaction closely akin to that found in teaching.

8. *Development of a visionary approach in program planning and construction.*

This is probably a bad phrase to describe a most desirable attribute of education. I am trying to point out that every element of an adult education program should lift the sights of the student, should take him to a new and higher plateau, should tempt him with the realization that there is more awaiting him either in the area he is studying or in other areas. In order for this to happen, courses and sequences of activities should be so planned and so taught or presented that the student's curiosity or desire to learn never flags. He should find in the work he does, in what he hears and sees and feels, new doors to open and ever more exciting paths to explore. He should capture the true concept of continuing education so that he returns again and again, so that his interests and enthusiasms broaden and deepen, so that he recognizes his role all through life as a seeker after more and more of the beauty and wisdom which the world has in store for him. This will not happen in every instance, but proper planning can make it happen much more frequently than we would ordinarily suppose.

9. *Provision for continuity of program.*

This puts added emphasis upon the long-range planning both for organization and program content. It is not enough to create a program which will run successfully for two or three years and then lose its momentum. A kind of organization is necessary from the start which will insure the steady and superior leadership in supervision and in instruction which make it a permanent part of the mores of the community. This implies assiduous care in its initial planning with an over-all view that looks ahead to added features and new activities as the years pass. It implies the involvement of people who will give their time for long enough periods to make results count and who will pass their responsibilities along to others like themselves without disruption of the program. It implies the kind of record-keeping and documentation which make each year's results a contributing factor to the next year's plans.

10. *Insistence upon financial independence as a goal.*

Here is a complicated and controversial aspect of adult education. There are some who feel it should be completely subsidized by government; there are some who feel it should be subsidized privately by philanthropies and foundations. Some think that public schools and colleges and universities should include its costs in their regular budgets just as they do the items of formal education. My own view, at least until such a time as we develop an entirely different attitude by the American people regarding the place of adult education in its life, is that it should sustain itself as far as is possible by the course and admission fees of participants plus whatever private philanthropic support it can muster to make up the difference. I do not favor its being offered free because the American people are inclined to belittle what they do not pay for. This is one of the unpalatable truths about why the teaching profession generally is so lightly regarded by the public. I would rather that people paid for what they received according to its worth and their capacity to do so. This still allows possibilities for scholarship adjustments and need not close the door upon those who are unable to carry their full share of the financial burden. Private philanthropy, largely local, should help to make up the difference. What I wish to emphasize is that, given time and care, adult education programs can reach a high degree of financial independence. A quality program will attract students and other participants in large enough numbers to make the financial problems capable of solution.

11. Regular and accurate interpretation to the public.

An all-important aspect of the development of a program of adult education is its interpretation to the community. There is little chance that it will be successful unless its receives the right kind and amount of attention from the press, radio, television, and every other regular medium of communication. There is little likelihood of success if the purposes and scope of the program are not accurately and attractively presented. Such presentation should be carefully planned by people who understand the nuances of this problem. There are people with these skills in every community whose aid can be enlisted. This should be done from the very start and should continue so long as the program exists. The program will grow in stature and in prestige as it has its quality spotlighted and as its details are explained again and again.

12. Adequate and objective evaluation of results.

One of the reasons adult education has had such difficulties in many places has been the inadequacy of its documentation and the failure to provide the means for ultimate evaluation of its progress. Admittedly there are some aspects which do not lend themselves readily to evaluation and others virtually impossible to evaluate. But there is a mass of evidence which it is possible to collect and which can give at least a definite indication of its worthwhileness. A good deal of the evidence is bound to be quantitative and therefore not so valuable, perhaps; it is entirely feasible, however, to make certain studies which will give some clues to the quality of what is being done. Class questionaires, audience reactions, and case studies are a few of the tools, and there are others which skilled people in a community can devise and use. Once again, as in the problem of interpretation, it is necessary to search in the community or nearby for people who can assist in this process. To achieve the fullest and most reliable kinds of evaluation, the techniques for it must be set up from the very start. Otherwise a partial and inaccurate picture of results will ensue. These techniques must be as objective as it is possible to devise, for otherwise the results will be discredited.

IV

There is more than promise and hope ahead for the many and diverse patterns of post-high school education. There is an impelling necessity. The leisure-time activities of increasing millions of our citizens, especially as they reach retirement age, the vast amount of time to be filled by housewives whose families have grown up and left the home, the minds of millions of men and women who do not go to college out of choice or circumstance as well as the millions who do—all these present ample material with which we can and must employ ourselves. Rightly or wrongly, America has the reputation of being a nation for doing rather than for thinking. Regardless of whether or not it deserves such a reputation, we know that America has tremendous need today as never before of the most creative faculties, the deepest insights, the most humanistic understandings on the part of all the people. New and proper impetus given to continuing education can do much to fulfill this need.

15

Broader Horizons for Interpreting Education

The primary function of the public relations person in an educational institution is to reflect and to interpret the seriousness of educational purpose in the new age, together with education's characteristics and problems.

* * *

The tendency in the development of the public relations function has often been to concentrate on the fund-raising, publicity, and other short-term aspects. Expert practitioners have been called in, frequently from previous experience in business and industry, to apply the techniques so successfully administered in acquainting the public with a product or an organization. To me this is a supplementary function to be preceded by the development of the public relations officer as something of an educational scholar. The first step in truly successful public relations would seem to be a sensitive awareness by the public relations officer of his institution's educational philosophy and a dedicated belief in such a philosophy.

(Address at the Far West District Meeting of the American College Public Relations Association, Santa Barbara, California, February 5, 1959)

I

IN SOME EDUCATIONAL CIRCLES CONNOTATIONS OF THE TERM "public relations" are anything but complimentary. There is still controversy and doubt about certain aspects of public relations work, to say nothing of the persistent difficulty of truly defining and giving respectability to the term "public relations" itself. Faculty and students alike have a way of using it as a label for anything which in their view smacks of appeasement, surrender of principle, the use of red herrings, or general puffing. At best, they consider it an evil necessary to the search for financial resources with mysterious techniques involving cocktail parties, chicken patty luncheons, and complimentary tickets to games. That wonderful street in New York, about which everything has been written but a song, has become part of campus folklore; and Madison Avenue is considered the spawning place or the original sinful manufactory for the emergence of this new species now being attached to every institution and masquerading under such guileful titles as "Director of Development" or "Assistant to the President."

Perhaps one of the contributing factors in this revulsion against the public relations function is the tendency to stamp every interpretive action or good will gesture with the "public relations" label. It seems to be almost automatically assumed that such moves are part of an insincere and purposeful pattern of ingratiation. People apparently find it difficult to agree with the concept that such occurrences may stem from an honest desire to be truthful and helpful. They appear to find it particularly difficult as soon as the term "public relations" is in any way associated with the action. It is a most unfortunate development as one considers the place of the public relations officer in the educational pattern.

There is no question that the search for respectability by public relations practitioners still continues, whether in the business world or in educational institutions, particularly in the latter. It is a phenomenon over which I have pondered for a long time in an effort to discover why it is so and how it can be changed. My analysis of those two questions may seem unoriginal. Truths have to be stated many times before they become widely accepted. In order to state these particular ones I shall try to offer first the background or framework within which I believe the public relations officer should be thinking.

II

We are entering a new age of education of which the paramount characteristic is a new seriousness of purpose. Each day there is increased realization that the role of education on the stage of modern society is more and more the central one. The American people, as never before, are moving steadily toward the full recognition that the quality of today's and tomorrow's educational process represents the basis for hope and for progress. Emerging from all the critical comments made in recent times and intensified by our sense of competition internationally is a deep concern for the proper encouragement and nurture of our youth. This is the heartening element that cuts through all the breast-beating, the finger-pointing, and the sometimes snide and unfair criticism.

A new feeling is developing that education is not designed to be merely fun, or a heterogeneous congeries of courses for study, or even a training device for the cultivation of vocational efficiency. It is rather that education has an underlying seriousness of purpose leading to the fashioning of broadly oriented, creative, and humane people all engaged in the pursuit of excellence and the fostering of individual freedom for themselves and their neighbors all over the world. It is a feeling pre-supposing the rigorous discipline that prevents any compromise with quality and insisting upon the complete integrity of those who teach and those who learn.

Other characteristics of this new and more seriously conceived pattern of education are easily discernible, also, if one examines what is taking place in colleges and universities today, at least in the more vital and dynamic ones. There is, first of all, a steady pressure toward increased responsibility on the part of the student himself. He is no longer expected to be the passive recipient of a fund of knowledge and ideas mainly predigested for him. It is rather demanded of him now that he fend for himself to a much larger degree; that he occupy himself with problems to which there are no pat solutions; that he move about more flexibly, more freely, and more restlessly amid the vast collection of intellectual and cultural samplings available to him; and that he look upon all this work only as a prologue to a continuing lifetime interest in the acquisition of truth and the appreciation of beauty.

There is, next, a lifting of the eyes beyond the boundaries of our own shores. The student is being guided toward the realization that the shrinking of his world puts him into new and more dramatic juxtaposition with his fellow man. He is suddenly perturbed about far-off revolutions, the rise and fall of governments, the clash of ideologies, or the scientific probings of another nation, not just in some detached and impersonal way, but with vividness and with deep sensibility of how these matters affect him directly. He has a new eagerness to live with other peoples, to roam to far places, to speak other languages, to savor strange cultures. This sense of adventure and discovery is as strong in him as it was in his seafaring and pioneering forebears, but his adventure and discovery are more largely in the realm of the mind. He knows already that the destiny of one nation, even a small nation, affects the destiny of all, sometimes subtly and sometimes broadly. He knows, too, that his personal destiny is inextricably enmeshed with that of the world. He searches, therefore, for those elements of an educational program that will prepare him for such a destiny.

There is also a steady groundswell of sympathetic attention to the more gifted student. He is now beginning to be lifted out of the tremendous numbers to be educated and recognized for his special talents. He is being encouraged to develop these talents to the fullest in recognition of his potential contribution to society. He is finding new ways open for him, ways that bypass the more traditional roads to learning. In more and more institutions he is being surrounded with specially designed curricula of an honors or directed study type. Through these he receives deeper and stronger stimuli from his professors and tutors and envisions some measure of his ultimate mission.

There is, in addition, the beginning of an outreach of the scientist and the humanist toward one another. The student who is scientifically minded is discovering that education is beginning to ask him to be a humanist as well. The liberal arts and humanities are finding an honored place in the science curricula. The student of the arts is learning that to live in this modern scientific world he must have broad conceptions of scientific knowledge. He is not as far as we should like him to be in this interdisciplinary exploration, but he is on his way. The world of the future will crumble without this kind of understanding, for it has created fantastic engines for destruction or enlightenment, depending upon the quality of the individuals who use them and the extent of their dedication to the needs of mankind. There is nothing new in the kind of crisis we face. We have merely lifted the level of the kind of crisis the world has created again and again and so have made its resolution dependent all the more upon the essential goodness of man.

One could point to still another kind of outreach, characterizing the new pattern of education. This is the outreach of educational institutions toward one another. Colleges and universities are beginning to discover that they can gain strength through regular association, whether formal or informal. They are learning that it is possible to share resources, to pool ideas, to intermesh faculties, to create joint curricula, to consolidate purchasing and other business practices. Through such co-operative approaches they envision a reduction in the duplication of effort and a sharing of experience that can be of tremendous mutual benefit. Thus, institutions either in close physical proximity or similar in type and objectives are drawing together and new associations are forming, such as the Association of Midwest Colleges (consisting of ten colleges in Wisconsin, Minnesota, Iowa, and Illinois) or the group of four in Massachusetts which is creating a fifth college. In a time when every educator is concerned over the question of providing faculty and facilities for the additional millions of students soon to make their appearance, this new attitude of co-operation is significant.

Finally, there is an unmistakably clearer awareness that the mind and heart of the student are equally important in the educative process and cannot be separated. Brilliant achievement can be the foundation for good or evil depending upon the values the student admires and believes in. As Horace Mann once said so colorfully, we are not eager to produce the "unscrupulous genius or the virtuous ignoramus." The core of learning is fashioned out of matters of the spirit as well as out of those of the mind, and if education is to be truly meaningful as a force in shaping a better world, it can ignore these matters of the spirit only at its peril. We always stand at a threshold of history, but each time we take a step, a door closes behind us, a pathway is denied us and we are led on inexorably in one direction or another depending upon the kind of people we are.

The problems growing out of the new age of education are as easily discernible as its characteristics and in some degree emanate from the latter. Lack of properly qualified teachers in sufficient numbers to staff the thousands of additional classrooms required for the relatively immediate future is, of course, a problem of top priority. The changes have been rung on all the ramifications of the problem time and time again, but the major issues remain unresolved. More money and more facilities are necessary along with more teachers, and here again we appear still to be only on the periphery of solutions rather than at their center. The general lack of acceptance up to this time of the broad use of mass media as tools in the teaching process in spite of repeated proofs of their efficacy under certain conditions is still another problem. We could list many more. Threading its way through all these is the disheartening time-lag that we seem never to adjust or correct. Yesterday's unanswered questions are already being superseded by today's and tomorrow's crop and we find ourselves bound in a bewildering chain of dilemmas.

III

This leads to what I think is the primary function of the public relations person in an educational institution. This is to reflect and to interpret the seriousness of educational purpose in the new age, together with education's characteristics and problems. It is, moreover, to interpret one's own institution in the light of these broad conceptual developments. In my view, public relations is the interpretation of an educational philosophy to all the publics who will be interested or concerned. All else is mechanics and technique, applied with skill and imagination and persuasiveness. While I would not minimize the importance of these, they are in the final analysis only ancillary considerations and are not difficult to develop and use.

The tendency in the development of the public relations function has often been to concentrate on the fund-raising, publicity, and other short-term aspects. Expert practitioners have been called in, frequently from previous experience in business and industry, to apply the techniques so successfully administered in acquainting the public with a product or an organization. To me this is a supplementary function to be preceded by the development of the public relations officer as something of an educational scholar. The first step in truly successful public relations would seem to be a sensitive awareness by the public relations officer of his institution's educational philosophy and a dedicated belief in such a philosophy. This presupposes spending much of his time in becoming familiar with the institution in all its ramifications, studying higher education generally, and eventually becoming imbued with a feeling akin to enthusiasm for both. It presupposes an agreement with and belief in what the institution is trying to do and therefore an ability to speak of such purposes and objectives honestly and unreservedly. In terms of action it means thoroughly grounding oneself in the history and progress of higher education, attending faculty and academic committee meetings as an observer, steeping oneself in every possible educational element of the college or university.

I can guarantee that two things will result from such an initial step on the part of the public relations officer. First, he will find that gradually his colleagues among the teaching faculty and the rest of the administration will come to look upon him with new respect and gratitude as they realize the depth of his interest and concern regarding academic matters. He will no longer be an outsider, but rather a full-fledged member of the fraternity, and because of his unusually objective position he will, if he tries, have a broader and finer mental grasp of the scope, the power, and the potentiality of his particular campus.

Second, the public relations officer thus educationally oriented will discover the conception of his own function to be changed. He will suddenly see that all his day-to-day tasks and problems together with the techniques he brings to bear upon them are tools of the educational process and can be interpreted with real educational significance. He will find himself devoting much more time to providing educational reasons for all the practical things his institution needs whether they be new buildings, funds from alumni, foundation grants, or good will from the community. He will be a co-ordinator in the finest sense of the word in that he will be the expositor of a total educational pattern and the means whereby the parts of that pattern become meaningfully unified. This will be his experience not only in his daily contacts with the world outside; he will be equally a factor in bringing the same kind of co-ordinate exposition to the campus itself, for here is where interpretation must begin.

When a man is given the title of "Vice President for Development" or "Director of University Development" it goes without saying that he is expected eventually to translate much of that development into tangible evidences such as buildings and money. The title also carries with it the more fundamental responsibility of being an active participant in the development of the more intangible educational structure. I recall that when I held such a post I spent months in organizing the faculty, the administration, and even the trustees into working committees whose function it was to grapple with the proper definition of objectives and the strengthening of curricula. Before setting my hand to the tasks of fund-raising and of evoking sympathetic support, I found myself persuading and cajoling the faculty into the creation of the broadest kind of statement on the purposes of a university—not just that university, but any university. They responded eventually with a magnificent and eloquent document which was debated up hill and down dale in all the schools and departments of the university until the degree of concentration upon the total educational process rose to new heights.

Later on, as head of an institution that was suffering from the lack of moral support from its alumni and that had virtually no alumni financial help, to say nothing of such a systematic device as an alumni fund, I recall meeting dozens of times each year and in dozens of places with alumni groups. In each instance, I talked almost entirely of our educational philosophy, our objectives, our innovations, our plans. Within three years after such an approach was initiated, we had an alumni fund to which almost thirty per cent of the alumni were contributing gladly; even more important, we had the good will of practically all.

I am not citing these as testimonials or models, for they are not particularly noteworthy, nor was my career in educational public relations particularly distinguished. They do illustrate why I insist that the public relations officer is primarily an interpreter of educational philosophy. His work starts from here if it is not to be shallow or meretricious. And when it does start this way, there are unmistakable educational reflections in all its facets. The news releases emanating from the bureau under his jurisdiction begin to deal more and more with the academic achievements and quality of the college or university rather than with social or personal matters for their own sake.

The spotlight begins to shine on research and scholarly publication as much as or more than on the fortunes or misfortunes of the football team. The intellectual discussions and cultural ventures of the campus are suddenly newsworthy. The speeches to Rotary or Kiwanis have a difference in tone and in motivation. The meetings of alumni are occasionally transformed from stag smokers or convivial dinners to discussions and seminars that are intellectually refreshing (and it would seem that this is as it should be when educated men and women get together). A passion for learning takes its rightful and preeminent place on the campus, and the public relations officer properly has a share in bringing about this mood and in conveying it to everyone who gives a thought to the institution.

It is the permeation of the educational philosophy into all the particular aspects of public relations work that makes this officer a co-ordinator. Whether he is planning the catalog, mapping the recruitment strategy, organizing the alumni, designating the tenor of "home town" stories, launching a financial campaign, creating a speakers' bureau, fashioning a public function, developing parent interest, or enlisting faculty sympathy and support, he uses the educational philosophy as a leaven and as a lever. In all this co-ordination he surrounds himself with a self-effacing quality and a willingness to involve others, not only in what they shall do, but in the credit they shall receive. His best efforts come in the time of his institution's prosperity and well-being for it is then that he makes clear the image that withstands the difficult circumstances, the stresses of adverse public opinion caused by unforeseen campus happenings, and the critical barbs of sometimes unreasoning attacks to which every college or university finds itself vulnerable. He is not the builder of that image except as any other faculty or staff member may be; he is rather the interpreter of what the college or university is and hopes to be. He is a master of strategy and tactics, but only after he has found a cause for which to fight.

The kind of task I am describing, therefore, is not for the journeyman. It is not for the fugitive from the advertising agency whose ulcers nag him to search for quieter arenas of activity. Nor is it for the loyal alumnus who has never quite found himself in the business world and yearns once more for the groves of academe where he can smoke his pipe and wear his tweeds in a euphorious aura of perpetual youth. It is not even for the faculty member who, disheartened and dismayed by the unwillingness of students to accept his words without challenge, seeks sanctuary behind the modern office furniture, dictaphones, and "incoming" and "outgoing" baskets of the administration. This is rather a task for the man who feels the hot breath of education's emergency upon him in almost searing fashion and who looks upon his college or university as one of the barricades thrown up against the tide of ignorance and spiritual bankruptcy that is a never-ending threat to survival. It is a task for the man with power, with patience, with pertinacity, with perspective, with prescience.

In finding broader horizons for interpreting education, the public relations officer is a key figure. With such a role he takes on stature and significance in the educational scheme of things. With such a role his academic respectability and his place in the sun cannot be successfully challenged for he is equal to his colleagues, a generalist and an expert, a philosopher and a practitioner, a searcher for truth in the best academic and intellectual tradition.